Wallace Library	DUE DATE (stamped in blue) RETURN DATE (stamped in black)

NORTHWESTERN UNIVERSITY STUDIES IN THE HUMANITIES
NUMBER FOURTEEN

NORTHWESTERN UNIVERSITY STUDIES IN THE HUMANITIES

NUMBER FOURTEEN

EDUCATION FOR JOURNALISM IN THE UNITED STATES FROM ITS BEGINNING TO 1940

BY

ALBERT ALTON SUTTON

AMS PRESS
NEW YORK

Reprinted with the permission of Northwestern University Press
From the edition of 1945, Evanston
First AMS EDITION published 1968
Manufactured in the United States of America

Library of Congress Catalogue Card Number: 68-54297

AMS PRESS, INC.
New York, N.Y. 10003

TABLE OF CONTENTS

CONTENTS

LIST OF TABLES

LIST OF GRAPHS

LIST OF MAPS

PREFACE

EDUCATION for journalism had established itself as a desirable member of the academic family and was taking its place alongside the older disciplines in American colleges and universities in ever-increasing numbers when this study was begun in 1940.

Although interested educators and newspapermen were certain of these facts, many other related questions remained unanswered. There was no reliable information on the exact number of institutions giving instruction in journalism or on the character of that instruction in the various groups of institutions offering the work. Concern was being expressed over the possibility that more graduates were being produced than were needed by the profession, and the feeling was quite general that many young men and women were not receiving the type of training necessary to prepare them adequately for careers in journalism.

Consequently, educators in journalism and the leading newspaper organizations in this country were giving serious attention to the problem of raising standards of education for journalism. This study was an outgrowth of their decision to sponsor a nation-wide survey for the purpose of bringing together significant information to clarify the issues involved in a program aimed toward self-betterment.

Most of the information included in this book was obtained from the questionnaires returned by representatives of four-year, degree-granting colleges and universities in the United States. Its accuracy necessarily is dependent upon the care with which the forms were filled out as well as upon that of the author in recording the material for presentation. Data have been checked and re-checked carefully in an effort to avoid errors, and the manuscript has been read and criticized by others interested in the study.

Although major emphasis has been placed upon an investigation and evaluation of education for journalism as it existed in colleges and universities in this country in 1939–40, considerable attention was given also to the origin of instruction in the various institutions, conflicting philosophies which arose, changes in curricula, and other aspects of the subject which help to explain the trends that have taken place in education for journalism from its beginning in 1869 until 1940.

Since the completion of this study, the entrance of our country into World War II has had serious effects upon education for journalism in our colleges and universities. Enrollment in most schools has decreased sharply, with practically all of the men being called into service; budgets in many institutions have been slashed because of reduced income; faculties have been depleted as staff members left to engage in various phases of the war; and, in general, curricula have been reorganized to meet new situations. Editors are searching for far more trained replacements than the schools of journalism are able to provide, even with accelerated programs under way

ix

which have reduced the amount of time required for graduation by twenty-five per-cent or more in most instances.

Today serious attention is being given to the planning of programs in journalism for the post-war period. When the war ends, thousands of young men will march back from the battlefields abroad into the colleges and universities of a nation at peace. Many of them will return to finish work that was interrupted by the war; others will be entering colleges and universities for the first time. All of the men who enroll in schools of journalism will be intent upon receiving the kind of training that will prepare them adequately and quickly for a profession whose demands will be greater than ever before.

Education for journalism will have to adjust itself to a new era. In meeting the problems that will arise, those charged with the responsibility of directing its course will need to draw heavily upon experiences of the past in shaping plans for the future. I hope that this book will serve a useful purpose by providing reliable information on education for journalism as it existed during the first seventy-one years.

To everyone who assisted me in the preparation of this book, I want to express my sincere appreciation. I am particularly indebted to Dean Kenneth E. Olson, Medill School of Journalism, Northwestern University, and secretary-treasurer of The National Council on Professional Education for Journalism, who encouraged me to undertake this study, made available the initial questionnaires that had been collected, and gave generously of his time in reading and criticizing the manuscript during its preparation.

Special mention should be made of the assistance given by Dr. J. M. Hughes, dean of the School of Education, Northwestern University, and by Dr. Louie W. Webb, professor of education, Northwestern University. I extend my thanks also to Dean F. L. Mott, School of Journalism, University of Missouri, who read and criticized the completed manuscript.

I am deeply grateful for the cooperation of all those who returned the questionnaires and answered letters sent out to gather essential information, without which this book would have been impossible.

ALBERT ALTON SUTTON

Evanston, Illinois
April 10, 1944

CHAPTER I

INTRODUCTION

NEED FOR THIS STUDY

EDUCATION for journalism has experienced rapid growth in colleges and universities in the United States since the establishment of the first recognized school of journalism in the year 1908. Many institutions of higher learning have adopted courses in the subject, and in a high percentage of these schools, instruction in journalism has become an integral part of the curriculum.

During this period of expansion, much confusion regarding the purposes and desired results of such instruction naturally has arisen. A lack of proper facilities and inadequate teaching staffs have been distinct handicaps in many instances. Such conditions have resulted in inferior programs, and as a consequence, the end-products have not always measured up to the expectations of the profession.

In the early stages of development, newspapermen expressed little concern over the type of instruction being offered, since few college graduates were entering the field each year. However, as schools and departments of journalism began to multiply, and editors were called upon to absorb a growing number of college-trained workers, their interest in the type of preparation given in the schools began to increase. As a result, the working relationship between leading newspapermen and educators in the field of journalism gradually became closer, and a feeling of common concern and responsibility for the training of future journalists in our colleges and universities arose.

This growing awareness of the problems involved in education for journalism finally led to the organization in 1939 of The National Council on Professional Education for Journalism. Represented on the Council are The American Society of Newspaper Editors, The American Newspaper Publishers Association, The National Editorial Association, The Inland Daily Press Association, The Southern Newspaper Publishers Association and The American Association of Schools and Departments of Journalism.

This Council was organized for the express purpose of studying the problems of education for journalism and of making recommendations aimed toward raising the standards of professional training.

Realizing the importance of first gathering complete and accurate information concerning the extent and nature of instruction in journalism, the Council began its duties by sponsoring a nation-wide survey of all four-year colleges and universities in the spring of 1940, under the direction of Dean Kenneth E. Olson, of the Medill School of Journalism, Northwestern University, who was secretary-treasurer of the organization.

When the National Council's plans for making the survey were under way, the author was invited to undertake this study, using the general outline which had been formulated as a basis. The work consisted of gathering missing data, bringing together a complete tabulation of information collected, and the specific organization, interpretation, and evaluation of the material utilized.

THE PROBLEM

The problem of this study has been to discover the types of programs being given in those four-year, degree-granting colleges and universities in the United States which offer instruction in journalism and to evaluate the various programs in terms of their provisions to carry on professional training in journalism, according to the standards set by the American Association of Schools and Departments of Journalism.

In order to answer the questions involved in this problem, many aspects bearing on the instruction being offered and the results, as measured by the absorption of graduates in the profession, were investigated. Questions which arose led to the collection of data on points such as the following: present organization of the program in journalism, the nature and content of the curriculum being offered, requirements for graduation and degree granted, the size and preparation of the staff of instruction, the amount and kind of laboratory equipment available for instructional purposes, the number of graduates turned out annually, the percentage of placements of these graduates within the field of journalism, and their distribution within the profession.

PROCEDURE

The information gathered in this survey was collected primarily by means of a comprehensive questionnaire, approved by The National Council on Education for Journalism, which was sent to 901 institutions of higher learning.

The list of institutions of higher learning published by the United States Department of Education served as a basis in determining what schools should be queried. From this list, all junior colleges, normal and Negro institutions offering less than four years of college work were eliminated, as were all professional and technical schools such as law, medicine, theology, music, physical education and others which by their very nature would not be expected to offer work in journalism. A final check of schools thus eliminated was made, however, and those which were found to be offering some work in the subject were added to the main list.

The resulting master-list contained 901 four-year institutions which might be expected to offer instruction in journalism. The distribution was as follows:

Universities and Colleges............................	662
Teachers Colleges.................................	164
Negro Colleges....................................	75
Total	901

Out of this total, reports were received from 896 institutionss or 99.4 per-cent. Repeated attempts to get responses from the five remaining schools failed.

As an initial step, the questionnaire and accompanying letter were sent to the 901 institutions included on the master-list. This was followed by a second mailing to schools which failed to answer the first inquiry. In some instances, further attempts were made to get the desired information.

Following a preliminary study of the questionnaires returned, letters and cards were sent out to gather data which were found to be missing in the blanks received, and catalogs were obtained from those institutions which failed to return the first questionnaire. In the end, sufficient information was gathered on all schools found to be offering journalism to give the data considered essential to this study.

In order to facilitate handling the material, the schools were divided into four groups, according to the type of program being offered. They are as follows:

Group A—Professional Schools and Departments of Journalism holding membership in the American Association of Schools and Departments of
Journalism.
Group B—Other Schools and Departments of Journalism offering degrees or
majors in Journalism.
Group C—Other Divisions of Journalism—usually within English Departments
—offering combined English-Journalism majors or strong Journalism
minors, representing substantial programs in Journalism.
Group D—Limited Programs offering from one to seven courses in Journalism,
usually carried as English department courses, in most cases being
counted on the English major but not constituting an independent
minor.

In deciding upon this method of grouping the various types of programs, there was no intention of attempting arbitrary classifications of the institutions concerned, and the group into which each was placed has been determined by the type of offerings made available.

RELATED STUDIES

Although several studies have been made concerning certain phases of instruction in journalism in institutions of higher learning, none of them duplicates the present study.

One early attempt at presenting data regarding instruction in journalism in institutions of higher education was that made by James Melvin Lee, of New York University, in 1918.[1] Appearing at a time when no school of journalism was over ten years old and few colleges and universities had included the subject as a permanent part of the curriculum, this study is valuable mainly from an historical standpoint.

[1] James Melvin Lee, *Instruction in Journalism in Institutions of Higher Education*. (U. S. Bulletin No. 21, Department of Interior, Bureau of Education, 1918.)

Directories published from time to time by The American Association of Teachers of Journalism and The American Association of Schools and Departments of Journalism in their official magazine also gave usable information concerning the number of institutions offering instruction and names of teachers directing the work. Since these studies were not restricted to all four-year institutions in the United States, the value in connection with the present survey was limited. However, material contained in *The Journalism Bulletin* for November, 1927,[2] and in *The Journalism Quarterly* for the years 1929,[3] 1932,[4] 1934,[5] and 1936,[6] proved helpful by providing information on education for journalism offered during these periods.

Izil I. Polson's study of the progress in teaching of journalism in colleges and universities, presented in a master's thesis at Northwestern University in 1924,[7] consisted largely of a review of early efforts made to establish the work and the author's own views regarding trends for the future.

DeForest O'Dell's doctoral dissertation at Columbia University on *The History of Journalism Education in the United States* contained some valuable information regarding the early beginnings but failed to present reliable statistics and data on recent developments. Thus, it throws little light on the problems raised in this study, except as background material.[8]

A study and analysis of the curricula of the twenty schools holding membership in the American Association of Schools and Departments of Journalism during the year 1926–27 were made by Vernon Nash in a thesis for the master's degree at the University of Missouri in 1928.[9]

Another study of education for journalism was presented by Nash in a doctoral dissertation in the Advanced School of Education, Teachers College, Columbia University, in 1938.[10] The author himself states in the preface that many of the "declarations are based chiefly or entirely on observa-

[2] "Journalistic Education in the United States, 1926–27," *The Journalism Bulletin*, IV, (1927), pp. 9–19.

[3] "Journalistic Education in the United States, 1928–29," *The Journalism Quarterly*, VI, (1929), pp. 1–4.

[4] "Directory of Teachers of Journalism in Colleges and Universities in the United States," *Journalism Quarterly*, IX, (1932), pp. 104–27.

[5] "Directory of Teachers of Journalism in Colleges and Universities in the United States," *Journalism Quarterly*, XI, (1934), pp. 110–40.

[6] "Directory of Teachers of Journalism in Colleges and Universities in the United States," *Journalism Quarterly*, XIII, (1936), pp. 226–50.

[7] Izil I. Polson, *Progress in Teaching of Journalism in Colleges and Universities of the United States and an Indication of the Trends Shown.* (Unpublished Master's Thesis, Northwestern University, 1924.)

[8] DeForest O'Dell, *The History of Journalism Education in the United States.* (Published Doctoral Dissertation, Teachers College, Columbia University, 1935).

[9] Vernon Nash, *What Is Taught in Schools of Journalism.* (Published Master's Thesis, the University of Missouri, Journalism Series, No. 54, 1928.)

[10] Vernon Nash, *Educating for Journalism.* (Published Doctoral Dissertation, Teachers College, Columbia University, 1938.)

tions, impressions and judgments, either of myself, or of others, or of both," which resulted naturally in many generalizations regarding the fundamental problems involved. In the present study, an attempt is made to base observations on facts collected from all institutions under consideration.

Norval Neil Luxon followed up the Nash curricula study of 1927 with a similar investigation in 1937, the findings of which were presented in an article in the *Journalism Quarterly*.[11] In this study, Luxon compared his findings with those of Nash and pointed out noticeable trends in courses and requirements over the ten-year period. Both of these studies dealt only with schools holding membership in the American Association of Schools and Departments of Journalism.

Valuable information also was found in books dealing with various·aspects of journalism education. Sara Lockwood Williams's *Twenty Years of Education for Journalism*[12] present a detailed account of the founding of and work done by the University of Missouri School of Journalism during the first two decades of its existence, and *Education for Newspaper Life*,[13] by Allen Sinclair Will, consists of a discussion of the Department of Journalism at Rutgers University. Both of these works emphasize the important part played by the press associations of both Missouri and New Jersey in establishing and forwarding instruction in journalism in their respective areas.

Likewise, Willard G. Bleyer in his *History of American Journalism*,[14] and Neil MacNeil in *Without Fear or Favor*[15] included information that was pertinent to this study. *American Journalism*, by Frank Luther Mott, which was published in 1941, also contains material dealing with education for journalism.[16]

Although studies and books mentioned made valuable contributions to the literature on the instruction in journalism in institutions of higher learning in this country, none of them attempted to solve the problem as set forth in this study. Each was restricted to certain areas within the broad field of education for journalism. However, the light which they throw on present conditions has been very helpful.

[11] Norval Neil Luxon, "Trends in Curricula in A.A.S.D.J. Schools," *Journalism Quarterly*, XIV, (1937), pp. 353–60.

[12] Sara Lockwood Williams, *Twenty Years of Education for Journalism*. (Columbia, Mo.: The E. W. Stephens Publishing Company, 1929.)

[13] Allen Sinclair Will, *Education for Newspaper Life*. (Newark, N. J.: The Essex Press, 1931.)

[14] Willard Grosvenor Bleyer, *Main Currents in the History of American Journalism*. (New York: Houghton Mifflin Company, 1927), pp. 426–7.

[15] Neil MacNeil, *Without Fear or Favor*. (New York: Harcourt, Brace and Company, 1940), pp. 378–87.

[16] Frank Luther Mott, *American Journalism*. (New York: The Macmillan Company, 1941.)

A more detailed account of the related material available in these works will emerge as reference is made to them in the chapters which follow.

Since the schools of journalism are the youngest of the professional schools in institutions of higher learning, the literature affording background material in the field of education for journalism is limited—a condition that is readily reflected in the comparative scarcity of secondary sources which could be drawn upon.

CHAPTER II

ORIGINS AND DEVELOPMENT OF EDUCATION FOR JOURNALISM IN THE UNITED STATES

EARLY HISTORY

THE first program of education for journalism in institutions of higher learning in the United States was introduced in 1869 at Washington College—now Washington and Lee University.[1] At least, the seeds were there, and during the intervening years, the growth experienced by this comparatively young member of the academic family has been surprisingly rapid.

Marked by a gradual spread of instruction through colleges and universities throughout the country, courses in journalism by 1940 had found their way into the curricula of over sixty per-cent of the nation's four-year institutions.

Today, thousands of graduates from these schools are engaged in newspaper work in this country and abroad, many of them in top-ranking positions of great responsibility. By preparing young men and women for this service, educators in journalism are fulfilling a mission envisioned by early advocates of professional training, who held steadfastly to the view that only through a better-educated personnel could the American press hope to meet adequately its tremendous responsibilities in an ever-changing Democracy. World-shaking events have helped reinforce this belief as the years passed.

General Robert E. Lee, of Civil War fame, at the time president of Washington College, is credited with having planned the first course of instruction in journalism ever to be offered in an American college or university. His plan provided for a system of scholarships for young men "proposing to make journalism their profession."[2]

The training was to consist of instruction in printing in a local plant, and it was designed to prepare students for service on newspapers of the time, which, for the most part, were operated by editors who also were practical printers. The student's editorial training was to be obtained while he stood before the type-case, composing his articles as he set them up in type. However, the scholarships were never used, and the plan as proposed by Lee, who thought it would be an important factor in the rehabilitation of the South, was abandoned in 1878.[3]

Despite the failure of this initial venture, the efforts of Lee had far-reaching effects. Newspaper editors and educators alike heard of the plan

[1] Lee, *Instruction in Journalism in Institutions of Higher Education*, p. 7.
[2] *Ibid.*
[3] O'Dell, *The History of Journalism Education in the Uinted States*, p. 17.

and began to discuss the merits of the proposal to include instruction of journalism in the curriculum of colleges and universities. New York City newspapermen became particularly interested. The *New York Sun* went so far as to send a reporter to interview General Lee, and there ensued a period of lively argument, with leading editors of the day divided in their stand on the issue.

Lined up in favor of the plan were such men as Whitelaw Reid, of *The New York Tribune;* George W. Curtis, of *Harper's Weekly;* William Penn Nixon, of *The Chicago Inter-Ocean;* David G. Croly, of the *New York Graphic;* and Joseph Pulitzer, editor of *The New York World*, whose interest was to crystallize later in a heavy endowment for the establishment of a school of journalism at Columbia University in New York.

Opposed to the movement were E. L. Godkin, of *The New York Evening Post;* Frederic Hudson, of *The New York Herald;* Horace Greeley, of *The New York Tribune;* J. C. Goldsmith, editor of *Frank Leslie's Illustrated;* William Hyde, editor of *The Missouri Republican*, and many others.

Arguments pro and con expressed by this distinguished group of American journalists—all leading critics of men and institutions of their time— helped clarify the issues, and these divergent views were weighed carefully by educators responsible for shaping the instruction finally adopted by early departments and schools of journalism.

Out of their thinking and that of other prominent newspapermen and educators emerged the philosophies of education for journalism which have guided its course and are definitely reflected in the types of programs being offered in present-day schools and departments of journalism in this country.

Eugene M. Camp, of the editorial staff of *The Philadelphia Times*, in 1888 collected the opinions of a number of leading editors and publishers on technical instruction in journalism for presentation in an address which he made before the Alumni Association of the Wharton School of Business of the University of Pennsylvania in an effort to interest that school in establishing the work.[4]

Typical of the arguments in favor of schools of journalism is the answer which was given by Joseph Pulitzer of *The New York World* to a query regarding the advisability of giving oral and written instruction in journalism. He commented as follows:

I see no reason why a chair in journalism, filled by a man of real talent and character, could not be made beneficial. Of course the highest order of talent or capacity could no more be taught by a professor of journalism, than could be taught the military genius of a Hannibal, a Caesar, or a Bonaparte, in military academies. Still military academies are of value, and so could a chair of journalism be made beneficial, if filled by a man of brains and experience . . . . The value of the idea would depend upon its execution.[5]

William Hyde, editor of *The Missouri Republican*, summed up the stand taken by many newspapermen when he commented thus:

4 Lee, *op. cit.*, pp. 9–10.
5 O'Dell, *op. cit.*, pp. 41–2.

I will say that one of the best schools of journalism is at the printer's case. Though not a printer myself, I have found it highly advantageous to acquire a tolerable thorough acquaintance with every practical feature of that branch of labor. But, above every other qualification, is a characteristic known as the "nose for news," by which is meant unwearying alertness and insatiable hunger for something "ahead of the other papers."[6]

Bolstering him in this position were the statements of Frederic Hudson, of *The New York Herald*, who made these remarks in answer to the question, "Have you heard of the proposed training school for journalism?":

Only casually, in connection with General Lee's College, and I cannot see how it could be made very serviceable. Who are to be the teachers? The only place where one can learn to be a journalist is in a great newspaper office. General Lee would have made a great failure if he had attempted to found a course for journalists in his university. College training is good in its way, but something more is needed for journalism.[7]

Emphasizing the need for a broad background of knowledge, J. C. Goldsmith of *Frank Leslie's Illustrated*, inferred strongly that such information could be obtained only outside a so-called school of journalism, thus overlooking the possibility of coördinating the social sciences with instruction in journalism, an integral part of which is in that very field in present-day leading schools of journalism. He said:

I believe our printers and pressmen correctly call me "the boy," so I suppose any scheme of education that I should lay down would be one of dreamy ambition rather than of experience. The books I read, or am always "going to read," are not many. Reid and Croly think of a school of journalism. I don't. Give the boy a good academical education, not omitting Latin and the modern languages, put him to writing wrappers on a large daily journal, and let him work up to the city department. That would make a Cummings of him, if it were possible to make another naughty but immense Cummings . . . . For style of writing, for form, strength and compression, study the broad-axe English of such men as Greeley, Corbett, Dana, Congden, Halstead, Godkin, Gibson, Swift, and White. If you would add something of personality, of "true inwardness," study John Henry Newman, Robert Browning's prose, if you can get hold of it, Thoreau, Carlyle, Tennyson, Shelley and Thackeray, not forgetting Light Horse Harry Watterson, who is a compound of Shelley, Steele, and Dick Swiveller. These writers have more or less *song* in them, and show you how to be personal without being an ass . . . .[8]

Basically, the two groups were in agreement that men and women entering the profession of journalism needed a special type of education for the work. Essentially, their arguments centered around the issue of whether the instruction given should be strictly technical in nature or should be broad enough to include important background material available through a study of the social sciences and other related areas in institutions of higher learning. Some of the men who were opposed to the movement held to the belief

[6] Charles F. Wingate, *Views and Interviews on Journalism*. (New York: F. B. Patterson, No. 32 Cedar Street, 1875), pp. 195–6.
[7] *Ibid.*, p. 130.
[8] *Ibid.*, pp. 109–10.

that colleges and universities traditionally were, and should continue to be, devoted to a "liberal" education, which to them signified an exclusion of any and all kinds of training aimed toward the acquisition of technical skills.

Furthermore, at that time, the apprentice-system for the training of printers and journalists was being followed, and many of the editors of the day had acquired their education in what they liked to term "the school of hard knocks." Starting out as a printer's devil, they had worked their way up to the editorial chair or to some other position of high standing within the profession. Consequently their reasoning, in many instances, was colored by their own experiences and by the knowledge that most of their contemporaries had advanced unaided by a type of professional training being proposed for colleges and universities.

In numbers, the opposition far outweighed the proponents for the new type of instruction in the beginning, and the objections they set forth undoubtedly had great influence in forestalling a rapid spread of the movement after it once had started. Likewise, schools that initiated programs of journalism despite these pressures none the less developed in a healthy atmosphere of sharp criticism—a characteristic which they of necessity were to instill in their graduates if they hoped to serve one of the primary missions of education for the profession of journalism.

The idea of teaching students of journalism the fundamentals of printing was put into effect by John A. Anderson, president of Kansas State College, at that institution in 1873, by establishing a course in practical printing. This department existed as a separate academic unit until 1916, when it was merged with the department of Industrial Journalism,[9] which today offers a strong program and is a member of the American Association of Schools and Departments of Journalism.

Several years before, however, Andrew Dickson White, first president of Cornell University, had urged the inauguration of courses in journalism in his institution, and an announcement of his intentions to give special instruction to "those who intend to make journalism their profession" was carried in his school's catalog as early as 1875-76. Although White's plan to offer courses in the subject did not materialize, some work was given in the form of special lectures.[10]

Teaching of journalism in the University of Missouri, a leading pioneer in the development of this type of professional training, began in 1878 with a course offered by Professor David Russell McAnally, head of the department of English. His course in the History of Journalism was the first attempt at a systematic presentation of the growth and development in this field, and a course in Materials of Journalism, started in 1884 atMissouri, shows the early attention given to practical procedures at this university.[11] This work finally led to the establishment of the school of journalism at the University of Missouri.

[9] O'Dell, op. cit., p. 21.
[10] Lee, op. cit., p. 9.
[11] O'Dell, op. cit., p. 36.

EMERGENCE OF A PATTERN

The distinction of providing the first comprehensive curriculum in journalism is held by the Wharton School of Business at the University of Pennsylvania, where the work was introduced by Professor Joseph French Johnson. The five courses listed in the 1893–94 catalog carried a total of eight credit hours. They were as follows:

1. Art and history of newspaper making.
2. Law of libel and business management.
3. Newspaper practice—exercises in reporting, editing of copy, conversation (sic!), etc.
4. Current topics—lectures on live issues in the United States and foreign countries.
5. Public lectures by men engaged in the active work of the profession.[12]

At Johnson's request, the work was known as "Courses in Journalism," not as a "school of journalism."[13] Inauguration of the program was mainly the result of the efforts of Eugene Camp, a member of the editorial staff of *The Philadelphia Times*, who had studied the possibilities for several years. His own views, and those of other leading newspapermen, given in an address before the Wharton School of Business at the University of Pennsylvania—mentioned earlier in this chapter—and his request that such a program be adopted are said to have been the deciding factor in establishing the work at this university.[14]

Whereas the work at Washington and Lee University and that at Kansas State College had to do with practical printing, for the most part, and the University of Missouri's first offerings concerned themselves primarily with literary style, the courses started at the University of Pennsylvania embraced a much wider scope of training, which, although more limited than most modern programs, compares favorably in many respects with the journalism curricula being offered in present-day schools.

Attention was given to both practical subjects and background courses. In this respect, the groundwork was being laid unknowingly for a course of instruction which has served as the pattern for many schools since then.

Before the end of the century, several other schools had established instruction in journalism, among them the University of Kansas, Denver University, Temple University, the State University of Iowa, Indiana University, the University of Michigan, and the University of Nebraska. Bessie Tift College, of Forsyth, Georgia, announced the opening of a School of Literature and Journalism in 1895, with fifteen courses listed in its catalog. However, no courses were offered during that year, and the department was not reorganized until 1923.[15]

By 1908, other schools added to the growing list included the University

[12] Vernon Nash, *Educating for Journalism*, pp. 14–15.
[13] Lee, *op. cit.*, p. 10.
[14] O'Dell, *op. cit.*, p. 46.
[15] O'Dell, *op. cit.*, p. 51.

of Wisconsin, the University of Illinois, the University of Oregon, the University of North Dakota, and Iowa State College. In 1912, the Department of Journalism in the School of Commerce, Accounts, and Finance was begun at New York University, under the direction of James Melvin Lee, who became a leading figure in the field of education for journalism.

The upward trend continued, with some schools expanding their courses into departments, following periods of experimentation. Interest on the part of newspapermen likewise increased as instruction got under way in several parts of the country, and state press associations began to lend active support to the movement in some localities.

The University of Missouri in 1908 opened the first recognized school of journalism in the United States. This school came largely as a result of the efforts of the Missouri Press Association, which had been directly responsible for the establishment of a chair of journalism at the institution several years earlier, and from that time forward had carried on a campaign for a regular school.[16]

In the years to follow, other schools were to be established as a result of the support of state press associations. Another notable example was the beginning of instruction at Rutgers University in 1925, which was a direct outgrowth of an annual Newspaper Institute of the New Jersey Press Association held at the institution, and came about through the efforts of the organization.[17] Other evidences of a close working-relationship between newspaper organizations and schools of journalism have been frequent during the life-span of instruction in journalism, and a feeling of mutual responsibility strengthened as the work became firmly established.

The purpose of this first school of journalism at the University of Missouri, as stated by Dean Walter Williams, was "to train for journalism—not to make journalists."[18] The curriculum provided for a practical approach to the problem.

Professional courses offered in the 1908 curriculum included the following: History and Principles of Journalism, Newspaper Making, Newspaper Administration, Magazine and Class Journalism, Newspaper Publishing, Newspaper Jurisprudence, News-Gathering, Correspondence, and Office Equipment.[19] The curriculum was fashioned closely after the one proposed some time before by Dr. Charles W. Eliot, president of Harvard University, in response to a request by Joseph Pulitzer, editor of *The New York World*, for his views regarding the advisability of establishing a school of journalism in some large Eastern university.

Great impetus was given to the movement for instruction in journalism in institutions of higher learning by the proposal made by Pulitzer in 1903 to endow a school of journalism,[20] and by his detailed position on the possi-

[16] Williams, *Twenty Years of Education for Journalism*, p. 3.
[17] Will, *Education for Newspaper Life*, p. 19.
[18] Williams, *op. cit.*, p. 53.
[19] *Ibid.*, p. 72.
[20] Bleyer, *Main Currents in the History of American Journalism*, pp. 426-7.

bilities of such a school given the following year in an article in the *North American Review*.[21]

The plan for endowing such a school was presented to Nicholas Murray Butler, president of Columbia University, and to Charles W. Eliot, president of Harvard, in the form of a pamphlet which was prepared on Pulitzer's order by one of his secretaries.

Although Columbia University became the recipient of Pulitzer's large endowment for the school of journalism, the views expressed by Dr. Eliot, of Harvard, and the program outlined by him for Pulitzer's consideration are significant.

Pulitzer recommended a program which emphasized editorial training in the collection and dissemination of news, with major stress placed on the social sciences. Courses dealing with the business aspect of newspaper publishing were to be carefully avoided. His intentions were made clear by these remarks:

> I am sure that, if my wishes are to be considered, business instruction of any sort should not, would not, and must not form any part of the work of the college of journalism . . . nothing, in fact, is more inconsistent and incompatible with my intentions or repugnant to my feelings than to include any of the business or commercial elements of a newspaper in what is to be taught in this department of Columbia College.[22]

Dr. Eliot, on the other hand, in the list of courses he prepared for Pulitzer placed stress on practical courses designed to prepare for the business department of a newspaper. The courses proposed by the Harvard president were:

1. Newspaper Administration (The organization of a newspaper office and functions of various departments and services.)
2. Newspaper Administration (Study of printing presses and other mechanical devices used in publishing.)
3. The Law of Journalism.
4. Ethics of Journalism.
5. History of Journalism.
6. The Literary Form of Newspapers (Approved usages in punctuation, spelling, abbreviations, typography, etc.)
7. Reinforcement of Existing Departments of Instruction for Benefit of Students in Journalism (Background courses coördinated with journalism.)[23]

This difference in emphasis regarding the philosophy upon which instruction in journalism should be based led to wide discussion. The attention that both of these men—each an outstanding leader in his particular field—lent encouragement to the spread of instruction in journalism and bolstered a widespread and growing faith among educators and many newspapermen in the soundness of programs for training in journalism. Of perhaps greater significance was the influence which these two somewhat

---

[21] *North American Review*, Vol. 178, No. 50 (1904), pp. 641–80.
[22] Lee, *op. cit.*, p. 13.
[23] Lee, *op. cit.*, p. 13.

divergent philosophies were to have in shaping the type of instruction to be introduced throughout the country with increasing momentum during the years to follow.

DIVERGENT VIEWPOINTS

Programs of journalism in the leading schools and departments of journalism today show the continuing effects of the views expressed by Eliot and Pulitzer.

The Eliot plan, which placed major emphasis on "practical" training, held greatest favor for many years. This fact probably was the result of two main reasons: first, proposals made by this leading educator naturally met with favor among school men; secondly, strong efforts were made to gain favor in the eyes of newspapermen, and it was felt that a close duplication of the work actually done in the profession would most nearly meet the demands made by editors upon newcomers seeking employment upon graduation.

However, the gradual trend toward less stress on technical courses in favor of background instruction in the social sciences points to a growing shift to the Pulitzer point of view. No doubt this can be attributed to a wider shift in the broader field of higher education itself, which has been in the direction of greater recognition of the need for a more thoroughgoing study of society and its needs in order to prepare individuals for meeting the growing problems in a complex and ever-changing social order. Instruction in journalism has not been alone in experiencing this change; it has taken place in many other areas of educational endeavor.

In most present-day schools, the curriculum of journalism consists of a mixture of the two philosophies, with the degree of emphasis varying from institution to institution. The distribution of weight placed on the two plans will be shown in the following chapters dealing with the four classifications of schools covered in this study.

This tendency of certain schools to favor one plan over another perhaps was due largely to the confusion which still exists in an interpretation of the real meaning of "vocational subjects" contrasted with "liberal or cultural studies"—a condition that has persisted for many years.

Many educators still regard subjects dealing with such things as business administration, engineering, household management, agriculture, law, printing and journalism as vocational; whereas French and German, and courses in the physical and social sciences and literature are said to be cultural in nature.

However, another group is in accord with the view that the purpose of a subject and not the subject itself determines whether it should be regarded as "vocational." Thus, as Theodore H. Eaton in his book *Education and Vocations* points out, "Physics would be a vocational study for the prospective engineer, Latin for the prospective teacher of Latin, and Floriculture for the prospective florist."[24] According to this view, any course taken by a student planning to utilize it in the field of journalism would be considered vocational. Yet, in many institutions of higher learning, the content of such subjects is the same for all students, and no direct efforts are made to adapt the instruction to varying interests and special needs of those who enroll.

Further confusion has resulted from legislative enactments by various states and from pronouncements by educational associations, defining "vocational" and "non-vocational" instruction in terms that set them apart, even when in purpose and in organization, or in content and method, a distinction is difficult to find.

Another opinion, widely held and firmly grounded in tradition, has set apart "pre-vocational education" from "vocational education." Even today, education designed to enable a student to discover the vocation he may desire to follow is said to belong to the pre-vocational field or to "vocational guidance," and it is so labelled in many colleges and universities.

Although less stress is being placed upon definitions of these terms—and more upon the actual needs of students—in present-day higher education, the traditional conflict still exists—a situation which undoubtedly accounts for many of the difficulties that have confronted educators in the field of journalism whenever changes that would lead to pointing instruction in new directions were attempted. The development of courses of instruction in journalism vividly reflects these divergent views in the field of education and the shifts that have taken place in the face of the resulting confusion.

As already pointed out, schools of journalism passed through a period during which programs were intensely practical and were guided almost entirely by so-called "vocational" objectives. However, there has been a gradual trend toward greater emphasis on "liberal" subjects, and in recent years most journalism schools have moved away from the strictly "vocational" objective. Today, they are organized as professional schools, providing students a broad cultural background in the social sciences, along with training in necessary technical skills.

As Izil I. Polson declares, the period from 1869 to 1908 was highly significant,[25] in that the first steps toward the establishment of education for journalism in colleges and universities were taken, and a growing feeling of the value of such instruction was developed throughout the academic world. Combinations of courses, and, in some instances, a single course served as experiments from which drafts for the more comprehensive programs were developed. The change in attitude on the part of many editors and publishers likewise was a great step forward, and opened the way for a

[24] Theodore H. Eaton, *Education and Vocations.* (New York, John Wiley & Sons, Inc.; London: Chapman & Hall, Limited, 1926.)
[25] Polson, *Progress in Teaching of Journalism in Colleges and Universities of the United States*, p. 17.

period of rapid expansion, marked by a quickening of interest on the part of educators throughout the country.

PERIOD OF RAPID GROWTH

The establishment of the first recognized school of journalism at the University of Missouri in 1908 gave new impetus to the movement, and announcement of the Pulitzer endowment of a school of journalism at Columbia University, which became a reality in 1912, likewise served as an added incentive to institutions that had begun to consider the idea of starting courses in the subject.

Although earlier reports on the number of schools offering instruction in journalism do not agree with some of the findings in the present study, because of differences in approach and other limitations, they do indicate the same general trends in that development.

An editorial in *The Journalism Bulletin* in 1927 declares that by 1910, one school and three departments of journalism had been organized: the school at the University of Missouri and departments at the Universities of Wisconsin, New York, and Washington. Less than 25 graduates a year were being produced by the four combined. In addition to these programs, one or more classes were being offered in journalism in Ohio, Nebraska, Cornell, Michigan, Indiana, Illinois, Kansas State, Pennsylvania, North Dakota, Bessie Tift, DePauw, Oklahoma and Colorado.[26]

All of these institutions were working under severe handicaps common to professional schools just getting started. At that time, no organizations for teachers of journalism or the schools and departments had been formed, there was no publication for those engaged in the work, and no textbooks on the subject as yet had been written. However, progress was being made, and as schools began to multiply, conditions gradually improved.

Dean Walter Williams, of the School of Journalism at the University of Missouri, prepared a report in 1912, based on a questionnaire sent to 200 colleges and universities in the United States, which showed that the following 32 institutions were offering some kind of instruction in journalism: Beliot College, the Universities of California, Colorado, Columbia, DePauw, Iowa State College, Universities of Illinois, Indiana, Kansas, Kansas State Agricultural College, Universities of Kentucky, Louisiana, Maine, Marquette, Massachusetts Agricultural College, Universities of Michigan, Missouri, Nebraska, North Carolina, Oklahoma, Oregon, Pennsylvania, Pittsburgh, North Dakota, Notre Dame, Ohio State, South Dakota, Utah, Washington, Wisconsin, New York, and Southern California.[27] Marquette University, Columbia University, and the University of Missouri had professional schools, and in seven others the instruction was given in a separate department.

[26] "Editorial," *The Journalism Bulletin*, IV, (1927), p. 25.
[27] *Ibid.*

In 1912, the American Association of Teachers of Journalism was formed, and the American Association of Schools and Departments of Journalism was organized in 1917. Both of these organizations, working in close harmony, assisted greatly in shaping and strengthening the new programs of journalism in colleges and universities throughout the country.

By 1918, the total number of professional and non-professional programs had increased to 91, according to a bulletin prepared for the United States Bureau of Education by James Melvin Lee.[28] The work was shown to be distributed among 31 universities, 17 state colleges and schools, and 43 endowed colleges and universities.

By 1920, some journalism was being offered in 131 schools, and of this number 28 were giving professional courses.[29] Ten were members of the American Association of Schools and Departments of Journalism.

A report for the year 1928–29 by the *Journalism Quarterly* on the number of students enrolled in 56 schools offering professional curricula, showed that 5,108 were engaged in the work in these institutions alone. No statistics were given on colleges and universities not giving what at that time were considered professional programs.

Commenting on the findings, the author of the report had this to say:

In the present tabulation of schools, departments, and curricula there are 56 schools. If these institutions are all to develop into Class A schools of journalism it is probable that there will not be need for more than three or four additions to the list during the next hundred years. Sixty Class A schools of journalism can easily take care of the needs of the profession . . .

. . . There is danger that schools already started may over-expand. A medical school does not consider lightly the matter of turning out one hundred or one hundred and fifty doctors a year. It considers itself with reference to the profession and with reference to the other schools and the needs of the country. . . .

There is no special trick to getting numbers and enrollment. The newspaperman has been getting crowds together all his life. The problem is more difficult than that of getting large classes. It is a problem of improving the schools and their products. . . . Improvement, properly considered, lies along the line of higher standards and carefully guarded enrollment.[30]

A directory of teachers of journalism in colleges and universities in the United States, published in 1932 in the *Journalism Quarterly*, showed that 667 teachers were offering work in 326 institutions. Compiled in the office of Professor H. H. Herbert, at that time secretary-treasurer of the American Association of Schools and Departments of Journalism and director of the School of Journalism at the University of Oklahoma, this list was based on an examination of over 500 college catalogs and returns from questionnaires sent to an additional list of 282 accredited colleges and uni-

[28] Lee, *op. cit.*, p. 16.
[29] Lee, *op. cit.*, p. 27.
[30] "Journalistic Education in the United States," *Journalism Quarterly*, VI, (1929), pp. 2–3.

versities in the United States. It included the names of teachers of English
who handled one or more courses in journalism. A table given in connection
with the report showed that the following changes had taken place:[31]

Date	No. Institutions	No. Teachers
1917	84	172
1921	171	276
1923	210	412
1929	190	436
1932	326	667

The directory for the year 1934 contained the names of 812 teachers in
455 institutions;[32] and another in 1936 showed that the number of teachers
had increased to 894 in 532 institutions.[33] These reports included junior
colleges in the list of institutions queried, and no indication as to the actual
number of strictly four-year degree-granting institutions was given. Furthermore, this survey did not cover all four-year institutions which might
have been offering work in journalism. Consequently, the report as given
in this directory, although valuable, was not parallel in its approach to
that followed in the present study, which covered all colleges and universities in the United States that might conceivably be offering journalism.

By 1940, 542 institutions, or slightly over sixty per-cent of the total
of 901 four-year, degree-granting colleges and universities which conceivably might offer programs of journalism, were giving some instruction in
journalism in this country (See Appendix A).

As may be seen in Table I, which is a tabulation of findings on dates of
origin reported by 415 of these schools, institutions of higher learning were
slow to adopt instruction in journalism. Although the idea started in 1869,
only 22 of the colleges and universities reporting had begun courses in the
subject by 1910.

During the period from 1910 to 1920, instruction in journalism was
started by 74 of these institutions; between the years 1920–30, 175
schools inaugurated the work; and in the last decade covered by this survey
—1930–40—144 schools began courses in journalism, despite a depression which led to severe curtailment in most institutions of higher
learning and the abandonment of many courses of study. (See Graph I.)

It should be pointed out that this tabulation includes only four-year,
degree-granting colleges and universities which were offering instruction
in journalism in 1939–40. Consequently, it does not take into account the
many schools which started the work and then discontinued it—schools
that were included in statistics of some of the earlier surveys mentioned.

[31] "Directory of Teachers of Journalism in Colleges and Universities in the United
States," *Journalism Quarterly*, IX, (1932), p. 104 ff.
[32] "Directory of Teachers of Journalism in Colleges and Universities in the United
States," *Journalism Quarterly*, XI, (1934), p. 110 ff.
[33] "Directory of Teachers of Journalism in Colleges and Universities in the United
States," *Journalism Quarterly*, XIII, (1936), p. 226 ff.

TABLE I

DISTRIBUTION OF DATES OF ORIGIN OF
INSTRUCTION IN JOURNALISM

Date	Accredited Schools	Other Schools or Departments	Other Divisions	Limited Programs	Total
1940				5	5
1939			1	13	14
1938		1	2	18	21
1937			3	15	18
1936		2	1	13	16
1935			1	15	16
1934		3	1	12	16
1933			3	11	14
1932		1	1	12	14
1931		1	2	7	10
1930		1	2	29	32
1929		1	2	13	16
1928		3	1	13	17
1927		3	1	7	11
1926		8	1	7	16
1925	1	5	3	16	25
1924		3	3	11	17
1923		3	4	10	17
1922		6	2	7	15
1921	1	1		7	9
1920		4	5	14	23
1919	1	2	1	8	12
1918			1	5	6
1917			1	1	2
1916		1		2	3
1915	2	2	1	5	10
1914	5		2		7
1913		2		1	3
1912	3	3		1	7
1911	1				1
1910	3			2	5
1909	2				2
1908	1				1
1907					—
1906					—
1905	2				2
1904					—
1903	1				1
1902	1		1		2
1901					—
1900					—
1899					—
1898				1	1
1897					—
1896					—
1895	2				2
1894	1				1
1893	1				1
1892	1				1
1878	1				1
1873	1				1
1869	1				1
Grand Totals	32	56	46	281	415

Although only 415 of the 542 institutions offering journalism reported dates of origin, the findings show clearly the widespread acceptance of programs of journalism that has taken place in colleges and universities, a majority of which today recognize instruction in journalism as an integral part of their offerings.

GRAPH I

GROWTH OF INSTRUCTION IN JOURNALISM IN THE U. S.
(Based on Reports from 415 Colleges and Universities)

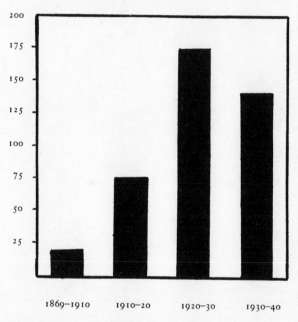

If these 542 institutions offering work in journalism were distributed equally among the 48 states, it would give an average of 11 for each state.

These findings point to the advisability of an inquiry into the question whether more schools may be attempting to train journalists than professional needs seem to justify. One of the purposes of this study will be an attempt to find an answer to this question.

Out of the 542 schools, only 103 were offering majors in journalism, and but 32 were members of the American Association of Schools and Departments of Journalism, entitling them to Group A ratings.

An analysis of the offerings in these schools shows the distribution by type of organization to be as follows:

Group A—Professional schools and departments of journalism........... 32
(Members of the AASDJ)
Group B—Other schools and departments of journalism offering degrees
and majors in journalism.............................. 71
Group C—Other divisions of journalism, usually divisions of English departments, offering combined English and journalism majors or
strong journalism minors—all giving substantial programs in
journalism... 55
Group D—Limited programs offering from one to seven courses in journalism, usually carried as English department courses and in
most cases being counted on the English major but not constituting an independent minor............................. 384
                                                                    ———
          Total... 542

In most of the early schools before 1908, the work was given only in the form of lectures, and, for the most part, it could not be considered real professional training, as judged by modern standards. Although several of the teachers had backgrounds of newspaper experience, their problem in the classroom was one of experimentation. As yet, no textbooks had been written by teachers of journalism, there were comparatively few reference-books on the subject and no prepared courses of study on which to rely. The choice of subject-matter, methods of approach, and the formation of a curriculum that met both the approval of the administration and a highly-critical press were primary considerations. These obstacles remained acute for several years to follow.

As Nash pointed out in 1928:

The Schools of Journalism have been thus between two fires. In many cases, per-haps most, they have had to fight a rear-guard engagement continuously within their universities while struggling to establish themselves in favorable regard of editorial offices. That the battle has been won indicates the intrinsic strength of the case for schools of journalism and calls for a tribute to those leaders, both in educa-tion and in the profession, who have been able to see beyond actualities to potentiali-ties and have therefore worked enthusiastically and untiringly in the field of profes-sional education.[34]

DEVELOPMENT OF CURRICULUM

As pointed out earlier, the curriculum offered during the first year at the University of Missouri stressed practical training along the lines set down by Dr. Charles Eliot of Harvard. Four years later, Columbia University opened its School of Journalism, in which the wishes of Joseph Pulitzer to exclude all courses dealing with the business end of newspaper publish-ing were followed.

[34] Nash, *What Is Taught in Schools of Journalism*, p. 27.

Dr. Ralph D. Casey, chairman of the department of journalism at the University of Minnesota, in an address in 1931 before the American Association of Schools and Departments of Journalism on the twentieth annisary of the first organization of teachers of journalism, indicated that the development of education for journalism might logically be divided into three phases. His remarks follow:

The beginnings of journalism teaching were experimental. Directors of departments, or perhaps I should say "instructors," as more consonant with their modest rank, were early occupied with building up courses of study, strengthening contacts with the journalistic calling, from which they had only recently departed, and finding niches in the faculty. Their more academic colleagues eyed the journalism teacher askance, sometimes with wondering and perplexity, and even occasionally with cool disdain, but as time wore on, with increasing confidence and friendliness.

The second phase of education in journalism was winning the respect of the newspaper profession itself. As the teachers trained graduates who knew their way about in a newspaper shop, as they associated themselves in the activities of state press associations, and freely gave service to journalism in many fields, a welcome was extended to them.

And then the third lap: editors and teachers sat down together at the conference table, to bring about the closest and most sympathetic cooperation between schools and newspapers and to arrive at a common understanding on problems relating to education in journalism.[35]

He pointed out further that the schools at that time had become an established part of professional training in the universities and that they had reached the point where massed attacks were no longer the fashion.

Many changes have taken place in course-offerings in the schools of journalism since 1908. Grant M. Hyde, director of the School of Journalism at the University of Wisconsin, speaking before the American Association of Schools and Departments of Journalism in 1936, after 27 years as a teacher of journalism, reminisced on the developments that had taken place as follows:

Then we didn't have a textbook to call our own—now we have a fair-sized library of specialized volumes. . . . From 1905 to 1915, a journalism teacher strained every nerve to be "practical." . . . We were trying merely to teach writing, the tools and tricks and techniques of the newspaper trade, the equipment needed by a cub reporter. That is as far as we saw our function. Some of us preached the desirability of a solid college education to supplement—or excuse—our technical teaching, and offered that as a reason for our operations.

Then about 1918, we began to see the value of the social sciences. . . . We made a great tumult about "background courses" and set up a curriculum containing more credits in social sciences than in journalism.

Then perhaps ten years later, we began to see that the social sciences were not accomplishing what we had hoped. The students were taking them in separate, unrelated doses, were locking them in an air-tight compartment like any other

---

[35] Ralph D. Casey, "Journalism, Technical Training and the Social Sciences," *Journalism Quarterly*, IX, (1932), pp. 31-45.

"college course," and were getting not the slightest glimpse of their application to journalism. We began to realize that our job was to show the students how to correlate these social science courses with each other and with the problems of journalism. Hence, we set up courses in "public opinion"—in "the influence of the press" —and we ourselves went prying into psychology, economics, sociology, political science, searching for the keys to accomplish this correlation.

Hence, now, in 1936, while listing in our catalogs an amazing array of specialized technical courses, we have really, in our hearts, reverted to doing what we so vigorously denied in 1910. We are admittedly becoming "theorists," and we are proud of it. Furthermore, the newspapermen are accepting us in this guise as they never were willing to accept us in the days when we tried so hard to be "practical"—our function is not to use university time to teach young people the things they can learn just as well in a newspaper office, but to direct their attention to necessary things they cannot—or probably will not—learn in a newspaper office.[36]

James Melvin Lee of New York University explained the tendency of early schools to emphasize "practical training" by pointing out that most institutions did not have the necessary endowment to make it possible for them to restrict their instruction to the editorial side alone and that they followed the Eliot plan for "practical" reasons of their own. Discussing the type of training being offered in 1918, Lee said:

> Technical courses in journalism vary from the single class in news writing at many of the smaller institutions to a well-rounded-out curriculum of several courses in the larger universities. At the latter will be found courses in such subjects as news writing, newspaper editing, newspaper making, newspaper advertising, current political topics, editorial writing, special-feature and magazine writing, short story writing, history and principles of journalism, etc. . . . Many of the state universities have technical courses in agricultural journalism and in the country weekly. At New York University special attention is paid to courses dealing with the editing and making of magazines, industrial papers, etc. Practically every institution has had to add special courses to meet the need of the field in which it is located.[37]

H. F. Harrington, at the time teaching at the University of Illinois, and one of the leading pioneers in education for journalism, in speaking of the type of training offered in 1919, wrote:

> . . . the difficulty all along has not been to justify the presence of the school of journalism—for this is a barren inquiry—but to adopt an effective program of instruction. Precedent has been lacking. Teachers have thus been privileged to act as pioneers in an untracked wilderness, and to arrive at a pedagogical scheme as experience gives assurance of success and issues warnings of failure . . . .
>
> It has been increasingly evident to many of us who have shared in this new movement that the most fruitful instruction in journalism is that which realistically duplicates the conditions of the newspaper office. Here is no make-believe, but the real thing. In other words, the project method which develops many journalistic prin-

---

[36] Grant M. Hyde, "The Next Steps in Schools of Journalism," *Journalism Quarterly*, XIV, (1937), pp. 35–41.
[37] Lee, *op. cit.*, p. 16.

ciples, as needed, in a natural setting of work pleasantly pursued, has proven best adapted to fulfilling the ends we have in view.[38]

The long article from which this excerpt was taken made no mention of the need for background courses in the social sciences, but rather it stressed the type of work done in the journalistic workshop at the University of Illinois, where the atmosphere of a real newspaper office was reproduced and students "learned by doing."

Eight years later, Dean Eric W. Allen, in an article in the *Journalism Quarterly*, expressed an opinion shared by many leading educators at that time when he said:

> If journalism means anything more than a mere trade, it must be based upon some depth of understanding. . . . The competent journalist must understand the scientific basis of current life, the complex of established principles that underlies any modern, objective, civilized discussion of politics, government, economics, psychology—in general, the art of living.
>
> Schools of Journalism will utterly fail of their deeper purpose if they do not attempt and succeed in producing a graduate who is thoroughly grounded not only in the separate social sciences, but also in the habit of keeping up with the authentic progress of the best current thought and actually applying the most enlightening conception of social science to his work as a reporter and as an editor.[39]

This view indicated a decided shift from the position taken by many leading educators of journalism less than a decade before. At any rate, it was an admission that not enough was being done in providing a background in the social sciences and an expression of the conviction that some efforts should be exerted in that direction. Since then, many of the best schools of journalism have striven for a balanced curriculum containing major work in both the editorial and business phases, with special attention also being given to typography. Even Columbia's school of journalism finally reached the point of including advertising in its list of electives—a move that was in direct opposition to Pulitzer's expressed wishes.

Nash's study of the curricula of the members of the American Association of Schools and Departments of Journalism in 1928 revealed that eleven schools, out of a membership of 20, at that time were offering a course in Contemporary Thought.[40] Ten years later, it was shown by Luxon in a similar investigation that 24 schools were giving courses in contemporary affairs, current events or public opinion, which represented an increase from 55 per-cent to 75 per-cent of the organization's membership.[41] The study pointed out further that in 1936–37, 42 undergraduate courses in

---

[38] H. F. Harrington, "Teaching Journalism in a Natural Setting: An Application of the Project Method," *Educational Administration and Supervision*, Vol. 4, (1919), pp. 198–9.
[39] E. W. Allen, "Journalism as Applied Social Science," *Journalism Quarterly* IV, (1927), p. 1 ff.
[40] Nash, *op. cit.*, p. 9.
[41] Luxon, "Trends in Curricula in AASDJ Schools," *Journalism Quarterly*, XIV, (1937), p. 359.

this classification, carrying a total of approximately 76 hours, were being offered, as compared with only 13 courses for a total of 47 hours in 1926–27. By this time, 16 schools were offering courses in current events or contemporary affairs; fourteen listed courses in public opinion; and six schools had courses in both classifications.[42]

Reports on course offerings in the present study will show the increased attention that is being given to background courses in the social sciences in AASDJ schools today.

PROVIDING A FIFTH YEAR

The American Society of Newspaper Editors expressed an interest in education for journalism in its first meeting in 1923, and pointed out the need for a working relationship between the newspapermen and the schools. Two years later, it adopted a resolution declaring that academic and professional training for journalism should consist of either a complete course at a school of journalism in some university leading to a degree, or attendance at such a school in a recognized institution, supplementing the regular college course. It went still further, stating:

> The Society commends as the ultimate goal of schools of journalism their development into graduate schools to the end that their educational standards shall be on a par with those maintained at the best schools of law or medicine.[43]

Since then, the school of journalism at Columbia University has been converted into strictly a graduate school, providing for a year of intensive study of professional journalism for students who have completed a four-year college program, and several other schools and departments of journalism have made provisions for a year of graduate work beyond their requirements for the bachelor degree. The Universities of Missouri, Wisconsin, Iowa, Stanford, and Emory are among those which have adopted such plans. The doctor's degree in journalism is offered by only one institution—the University of Missouri.

Although the programs in operation at Iowa, Stanford, and Emory University (which announced a five-year plan in 1941) are called five-year plans, the work they are doing appears to differ little from that being carried on at such schools as Missouri, Wisconsin and Minnesota, where a fifth year leading to a master's degree is provided for students who have earned the bachelor's degree in journalism or its equivalent.

Northwestern University's Medill School of Journalism was the first school to break away entirely from the traditional sequence by setting up a five-year plan for professional training, modelled after that of the law schools, which leads to the master of science degree in journalism—the only degree offered by this school.

42 *Ibid.*, p. 360.
43 Kenneth E. Olson, "Schools of Journalism and the Press," *Journalism Quarterly*, XVI, (1939), p. 32.

The five-year plan at Northwestern University, inaugurated in 1938, aims to provide students with a broad background in English, economics, history, political science, sociology, and commerce, in addition to sound professional training under seasoned teachers with wide newspaper experience. Like schools of law, the Medill School of Journalism requires three years of college work for admission to the professional courses. In the fourth year, while continuing background courses, students begin their professional studies, which makes them eligible at the end of the first professional year for either the degree of Bachelor of Science, conferred by the College of Liberal Arts, or the degree of Bachelor of Science in Commerce, conferred by the School of Commerce. Concentration on professional courses comes in the fifth year, and students who satisfactorily complete this program receive the Master of Science in Journalism as a professional degree.[44]

The entrance of this country into war in December, 1941, naturally had rather serious effects on graduate enrollments in schools of journalism throughout the country, since practically all men students in the fourth and fifth years were within the Selective Service age-limits, and many of these men were called immediately for active duty.

Consequently, some revisions aimed toward making it possible for men to obtain degrees in journalism before being called for military duty were necessary. At Northwestern University, for instance, work leading to a Bachelor of Science degree in journalism was reestablished and the curriculum was adjusted so that students could complete work on this degree in three years by utilizing the summers. However, the graduate program was retained, and all students who were able to continue for the Master's degree were encouraged to do so.

Much of the improvement in the curricula and in education for journalism as a whole came through the work of two national organizations now serving teachers and schools of journalism—the American Association of Schools and Departments of Journalism and the American Association of Teachers of Journalism.

ATTEMPTS TO RAISE STANDARDS

The American Association of Teachers of Journalism, organized in 1912, began its activities four years after the opening of the first school of journalism. Only one of the men who attended the first conference of the organization—Grant M. Hyde, director of the School of Journalism, University of Wisconsin, still is engaged in the work.[45]

The American Association of Schools and Departments of Journalism, which was started in 1917, was formed by 10 universities in which instruction had been well-developed. Charter members were: Missouri,

[44] *Catalog* (Medill School of Journalism, Northwestern University, 1939–40), p 14.
[45] Lawrence W. Murphy, "Professional and Non-Professional Teaching of Journalism," *Journalism Quarterly*, IX, No. 1 (1932), p. 46.

Wisconsin, Columbia, Kansas, Ohio State, Oregon, Texas, Montana State, Washington, and Indiana. By 1940, the membership in this organization had increased to 32 schools, representing 25 states.

These two groups met together for the first time in 1921 at the third session of AASDJ. Although remaining separate organizations, they have worked in close harmony since that time.

Need for some method of classification of schools and departments of journalism was felt as the number of institutions offering the work began to increase, and trial classifications were made as early as 1920. Requirements set up in the original constitution of the AASDJ to regulate entrance of new members read as follows:

1. Instruction in journalism must be organized as a seperate academic unit, such as a school or department of journalism, with a journalism faculty of at least two full-time teachers of the rank of instructor.

2. Entrance requirements to the academic unit must be at least 14 units of approved secondary school work, or graduation from a secondary school accredited by the state universty.

3. Education in preparation for journalism must consist of a four-year collegiate course, at least two years of which shall include professional courses in journalism, and be spent in residence.

4. The majority of students enrolled in the academic unit (school or department of journalism) must be regular candidates for a bachelor's (or master's) degree.

5. Instruction in journalism must include 24 units or semester hours (on the basis of 120 units required for the bachelor's degree) in professional courses in journalism, which shall include at least (1) six units of reporting or news writing, (2) three units in copy reading, (3) two units in editorial writing, and (4) two units in the history and principles of journalism.

6. Instruction in professional courses must include laboratory work of a practical kind, done under the immediate direction of instructors in journalism.

7. A complete course in preparation for journalism must be organized and all the work outlined in the fifth sub-section of this section shall have been given at least one year, before an institution shall be eligible for membership.[46]

In 1923, the AASDJ provided for a Council on Education in Journalism, whose purpose was to be that of formulating and maintaining standards of journalistic education and the classification of schools and departments of journalism in accordance with such standards.[47] The next year, the Principles and Standards of Education for Journalism formulated by this Council were adopted. Based on the original rules contained in the constitution of the AASDJ, the new standards were broader in scope and provided for a stiffening of requirements. Since then, several revisions and additions have been made, the latest resulting in a new list of Proposed Standards for Schools of Journalism, which was approved in principle at the meeting of

---

[46] *Rules and Precedents of the National Council on Education for Journalism* (Mimeographed bulletin prepared by chairman of the Council in October, 1938).
[47] *Ibid.*

the two organizations in December, 1940. After revisions, these new standards were approved by the convention of the AASDJ at Des Moines, Iowa, on December 28, 1941.

A comparison of the new standards with those first set forth in 1917 shows that several changes have been made, and indicates the direction and extent of progress that has been made in improving the quality of professional training considered necessary for Group A rating since that time. The new Revised Standards are as follows:

1. Instruction in professional schools and departments of journalism shall seek to educate men and women of ability for responsible positions in the field of journalism and for service to the public and the profession. Educational standards shall be maintained on a level with those in other fields of professional training.

2. Such instruction in journalism shall be organized as a separate academic unit with a minimum faculty of three full-time teachers of journalism of professorial rank. The term "professorial rank" shall be interpreted to mean the ranks of assistant professor, associate professor, and professor.

Academic and professional training shall consist of a complete course leading to a recognized degree. The institution of which the school or department is a member shall be of recognized standing.

Requirements for admission to and graduation from the school or department of journalism shall be such as to maintain the educational standards for journalistic instruction as high as those in other fields of professional training at the institution of which the school or department is a part. Professional courses in journalism in institutions of higher learning that have no regularly established school or department of journalism are disapproved as education for the profession of journalism.

3. Members of the faculties of schools and departments of journalism engaged to teach technical courses in journalism shall have had adequate professional training in the field (five years as a minimum recommended) before their appointment as instructors; those responsible for instruction in graduate courses shall have had, in addition, sufficient advanced academic training or professional experience to equip them to teach such courses on the same level of competency as exists in other disciplines.

4. Distinctly professional courses shall be open only to students who have completed successfully at least two full years of a regular four-year or five-year course in the school or department of journalism, except that orientation courses and an introductory course in journalistic writing and reporting may be offered as lower division courses.

5. It is recommended that the bachelor's and master's degrees be so designated as to indicate that graduates have completed a major in professional journalism subjects.

6. The four-year course leading to the bachelor's degree in journalism shall normally include, in addition to professional courses in journalism, a suitable and related selection of courses in history, economics, government and politics, sociology, literature and English composition, natural science, foreign languages, psychology, and philosophy, or adequate groupings of these disciplines.

7. The completion of four years of work in a university or college, consisting of not fewer than 120 semester or 180 quarter units, shall be required for the bachelor's degree with a major in journalism.

8. Schools and departments of journalism shall provide such scholastic standards

or such personnel-testing techniques as may have validity for the selection of major students. Accepted guidance procedures shall be used in advising students admitted as majors.

9. At least four-fifths of the students enrolled in professional courses in the school or department shall be regularly enrolled candidates for bachelor's or advanced degrees.

10. The basic professional courses in journalism shall afford instruction and practice under competent and experienced instructors in reporting, news editing, editorial and interpretative writing, magazine writing and editing, typography and make-up, and law of the press; and instruction in advanced courses dealing with the relationship of the press to government and society (history of journalism, press and foreign affairs, press and public opinion, comparative journalism, ethics, influence of the newspaper, etc.).

11. Courses in advertising, circulation, business management, radio writing and production, and pictorial journalism, as well as in other fields of journalism, shall be offered only when the teaching personnel has the necessary experience and training in the specialized fields to conduct such work competently, and only when the school or department of journalism has the necessary laboratory facilities with which to conduct such work.

12. Students shall not receive credit for practical journalistic work unless such work is done under the direct supervision of a competent instructor in journalism as a part of a regular course in journalism.

13. The number of instructors in journalism shall be sufficient to insure careful attention to the individual needs of students, and the amount of class and laboratory work required of each instructor shall not exceed that of instructors in comparable disciplines.

14. Instructors shall be encouraged to carry on research work and to contribute to the literature of journalism.

15. Adequate library facilities comparable with those available in other professional disciplines shall be available for use of the students. These facilities shall include adequate contemporary and historical files of newspapers and periodicals, documentary materials, and a wide range of books and treatises in the various fields of journalism.

16. Sufficient laboratory equipment shall be available in the school or department to train students in the production methods of various forms of journalism under study.

17. A complete course in preparation for journalism shall have been organized in accordance with the foregoing, and the professional courses outlined shall have been given for at least three academic years in accordance with these regulations before an institution shall be eligible for an invitation to membership in the American Association of Schools and Departments of Journalism.[48]

Tightening of requirements and the elevation of standards for instruction in journalism did not come alone from the educational organizations interested in professional training. Newspaper groups in recent years have played an important part.

[48] Copy of new Revised Standards approved by the AASDJ at the 1941 meeting in Des Moines, Iowa, which will replace the old standards in the Constitution.

In 1928, the American Society of Newspaper Editors' committee on schools of journalism pointed out the need for adequate classification of schools, departments, and courses in journalism, and in its report to the Society on April 12, 1930, the chairman, George B. Armstead, of the *Hartford Courier*, declared:

It is the opinion of your committee that schools of journalism should be graduate schools, as are the good schools of law and medicine. It seems a mistake to push trade school subjects into the academic college curriculum and by so doing seriously abbreviate the academic work. . . .

Your committee would recommend that this society seriously consider urging that departments of journalism be graduate schools. Ought we not to ask that they demand of the boys a thorough academic training before coming to the journalism teachers for instruction in shop practice, in the history of newspapers, in dramatic criticism, book reviewing and such subjects?[49]

M. V. Atwood, of the Gannett Newspapers, another member of the committee, took a somewhat different stand. He questioned the willingness of a young man to invest in his education for journalism the sum that would be required, when faced with the knowledge that pay in the profession is low as compared to remuneration that could be expected from law or medicine. He said:

Under this system I fear we would get training only for managing editors and public relations counsels. And you cannot make a newspaper, any more than you can fight a war, without buck privates in the rear ranks. . . .

Journalism education, it seems to me, has two distinct sides. One is purely technical, whereby a person is taught the technicalities of news writing, headlines, and makeup. Obviously this must be learned in some way. Formerly a fairly good job was done on the newspapers by the apprentice system. But as industry has been speeded up, the apprentice system has been breaking down. And I am afraid that on few papers with six or seven editions daily, and many members of the staff "doubling in brass," there is much time for pedagogy. It does seem as if there ought to be some way in a school for real newspapermen who do have the gift for teaching—and I am convinced that teaching is largely a gift—to give this training. The other side, of course, as far as the professional aspects of journalism are concerned, is the most important. It is giving the newspaper worker a solid background of information on the many topics with which newspapers deal.

In view of this situation, might it not be a good plan for the present to work with the schools and departments of journalism in some way to the end that the chief emphasis shall be placed on the essentials, but at the same time young men and women shall be exposed, at least, to the technique, through practiced and qualified editor-teachers? . . .

I believe that a score or even a dozen schools or departments of journalism would be ample to take care of the demand. Then if the informative and cultural courses in these schools could be taught by scholars, and the technical side by men who really know newspaper writing, headlines and makeup, I care not how hard-boiled or

[49] "The Report of the Committee on Schools of Journalism to the A.S.N.E.," *Journalism Quarterly*, VII (1930), pp. 145–6.

profane they may be, I am inclined to believe we might get somewhere. Too many who are teaching technique now do not "know their stuff."[50]

Here, in this meeting, conflicting views were expressed by these two members of the same committee, which indicated that a lively interest in education for journalism was developing. Furthermore, in their remarks were contained some of the pressing issues that for many years have confronted educators and others striving to determine the most desirable program for professional schools of journalism.

Following the convention of the AASDJ and the AATJ in Boston in 1930, Fred Fuller Shedd, then president of the A.S.N.E., initiated the organization of a Joint Committee which was to include representatives of the principal newspaper associations and representatives of the schools of journalism for the purpose of studying the problems of education for journalism.[51]

This committee was composed of the following national organizations: the American Association of Schools and Departments of Journalism, represented by Dr. W. G. Bleyer, of the University of Wisconsin, Dean F. L. Martin, of the University of Missouri, and Dean Eric W. Allen, of the University of Oregon; the American Association of Teachers of Journalism, represented by Franklin Banner, of the Pennsylvania State College, John E. Drewry, of the University of Georgia, and Allen S. Will, of Columbia University; the American Society of Newspaper Editors, represented by Fred Fuller Shedd, editor of the Philadelphia *Evening Bulletin*, Paul Bellamy, managing editor of the Cleveland, Ohio, *Plain Dealer*, and H. B. Johnson, editor of the Watertown, New York, *Daily Times;* the National Editorial Association, represented by George C. Dollivar, editor of the Battle Creek, Michigan, *Moon Journal*, Lemuel E. Hall, editor of the Wareham, Massachusetts, *Courier*, and Walter D. Allen, Brookline, Massachusetts.[52]

At its first meeting, on April 4, 1931, in Cleveland, the joint committee passed a resolution declaring the necessity for better cooperation between newspapers and schools of journalism both in the placement of graduates and in each other's activities, and it unanimously endorsed the standards of education for journalism of the AASDJ, pointing out the necessity of sufficiently high standards for graduation from all schools and departments of journalism "to prevent students who are lacking in knowledge, ability or proficiency from obtaining an academic degree in journalism."

Touching upon the type of training needed, the resolution declared:

We recognize the increasing demand of newspaper organizations for college trained workers. We believe it the proper mission and obligation of the schools of journalism to supply that demand. And to that end we believe that the basic education for newspaper work should be in such courses as are generally recognized for

[50] *Ibid.*, p. 151.
[51] Olson, *op. cit.*, p. 33.
[52] "News Notes," *Journalism Quarterly*, VIII (1931), p. 305.

the bachelor's degree specifically directed and applied so far as possible to the problems of newspaper service. We believe that such college training, so directed, should be supplemented by specific instruction in the fundamentals of newspaper service, its mission and obligations, its history, its ethics, with special regard for the definition and development of news and in the practical art of newspaper work with laboratory equipment to afford training and practice for the small papers as well as the large.[53]

The committee voted also to recommend to its parent organizations "the taking of steps toward having a study made on the standards and methods of the schools of journalism and of the requirements on the part of newspapers from the standpoint of these schools."[54] This study also was to include a review of the opportunities in newspaper service for graduates of schools of journalism.

By the time of the second meeting of this committee in December, 1931, which was held in Minneapolis, the A.S.N.E. and the N.E.A. had adopted resolutions endorsing the plan, and the Inland Daily Press Association had agreed to it. At a third meeting in Cleveland in May, 1932, representatives of the American Newspaper Publishers Association joined with representatives of N.E.A. and A.S.N.E. in considering the committee's problems.[55]

The deepening of the depression, accompanied by the financial problems which all newspapers encountered, made it impossible to get the committee together for another meeting until January 20–21, 1939. However, during this lapse of time, work continued in an effort to reach the final objective of obtaining the endorsement of all of the leading newspaper organizations.

When Dean Kenneth E. Olson, of the Medill School of Journalism, Northwestern University, became president of the AASDJ in 1938, he made a vigorous drive to accomplish this end, and largely through his efforts formal approval had been obtained by June, 1938, from five major newspaper associations: The American Society of Newspaper Editors, The National Editorial Association, The American Newspaper Publishers Association, The Southern Newspaper Publishers Association, and The Inland Daily Press Association.

Plans for the first meeting of this enlarged group, to be held in Chicago on January 20–21, 1939, were announced by Dean Olson before a meeting of the AASDJ and the AATJ in Topeka in December, 1938. Expressing great satisfaction over the progress that had been made, he said:

Out of this new movement I hope there may come the approval by the major newspaper organizations of this country of definite standards for our schools and official recognition of the schools which meet those standards as the professional schools serving the American press. Inevitably that must mean a classification of our

[53] *Ibid.*
[54] *Ibid.*, p. 306.
[55] Olson, *op. cit.*, p. 34.

schools and the development of some practical plan for the recognition and employment of our graduates.

. . . I think we must face the criticisms that are being made of our schools fairly and squarely and attempt to bring our educational programs in line with what the press demands. Editors and publishers with whom I have talked during the past year profess dissatisfaction with our programs; but few of them know anything about what we are doing. Most newspapermen who have not had contact with schools of journalism cling to the outmoded idea that we pre-empt the whole of our students' time with technical courses. Many of them still believe that a journalism student spends four years studying reporting, copyreading, and other trade-school courses and as a result does not have time to get the broad general education he needs. Much of this criticism that is now being levelled at our schools is based upon this ignorance of our programs. . . . I believe that one of our greatest needs right now is to educate newspaper critics as to what we are doing.[56]

The National Council on Professional Education for Journalism, established in 1939, was a direct outgrowth of the Joint Committee. Organizations represented on the Council are the same groups which had places on the Joint Committee. Officers of the Council at the present time (1941) are: Jerome D. Barnum, publisher of the Syracuse *Post-Standard*, chairman; Walter Allen, publisher of the Brookline (Mass.) *Chronicle*, vice-chairman; and Dean Kenneth E. Olson, of the Medill School of Journalism, Northwestern University, secretary-treasurer. Caspar Yost, for many years chief editorial writer of the *St. Louis Globe-Democrat*, and the founder and first president of The American Society of Newspaper Editors, played a leading part in the formation of the Council and was its first chairman. As early as 1924, he had made a plea for close cooperation between newspaper organizations and schools of journalism. His firm belief in the value of strong journalism schools was expressed at that time in these words:

The schools of journalism, in short, must be increasingly relied upon as the sources of supply from which the ranks of journalism are to be recruited. Following the same road over which the other and older professions have traveled, it must eventually reach the point where for its own protection it will set up definite standards of qualification for admission to practice. . . . Educational preparation is as requisite to success in journalism as in other professions.[57]

Before his death in 1940, he saw many of his proposals put into effect and a gradual strengthening of journalism schools throughout the country.

Herbert M. Davidson, chairman of the 1940–41 Schools of Journalism Committee of the Southern Newspaper Publishers Association—an organization whose interest in education for journalism is of long standing—commented as follows about the activities of the National Council on Professional Education for Journalism after two years of service on it:

[56] Olson, *op. cit.*, pp. 34–5.
[57] Caspar S. Yost, *The Principles of Journalism* (New York: D. Appleton and Company, 1924), pp. 72–3.

While progress to date may not seem sensational, every meeting of the Council has led us a step nearer its goal. Every member of the Council—and since its organization there have been few changes in personnel—seems inspired with the importance of our task and willing to sacrifice any amount of time and effort to forward the work. It is natural that the representatives of leading schools of journalism should take an avid interest in the problems with which the Council is trying to deal, but you will be interested and delighted to learn that the representatives of newspaper organizations are equally enthusiastic.[58]

Evidence of the Council's desire to expand its usefulness was shown in its meeting in New York on December 30, 1940, when the group voted to extend invitations to the American Association of Advertising Agencies and to the Periodical Publishers Association as soon as a definite enough program is developed and when the committee feels that the time is appropriate.

The purpose of the National Council on Professional Education for Journalism is to study the problems of education for journalism and of raising the standards of instruction in this field. One of its first moves was the sponsorship of a nation-wide survey of all four-year colleges and universities to determine the extent and nature of instruction in journalism in the United States, and the degree of absorption of graduates of journalism in all journalistic fields. Findings obtained will be presented in the following chapters of this study.

With a view toward raising the standards of professional schools of journalism to a point where they are equal in quality to the schools of law and medicine, the major newspaper organizations in conjunction with educators of journalism have launched out definitely on a broad program of self-betterment, the realization of which they are confident will come through closer cooperation in drafting a program for training young men and young women who will direct the future destinies of the American press.

General Lee, Joseph Pulitzer, and Dr. Charles W. Eliot had a similar vision years ago when education for journalism was in its infancy. The progress that has been made since then, despite many handicaps and discouragements along the way, perhaps is an indication of the advancement that may be expected during the years to come. At least, leading editors and publishers of the nation are ready and anxious to help point the future course of education for journalism, as is evidenced by their growing interest in learning more about the extent and nature of such instruction and in efforts being directed toward accreditation of only those schools equipped and able to offer the highest type of professional training for journalism.

NATURE OF CHANGES

Out of the early attempts to establish education for journalism in institutions of higher learning, two conflicting philosophies emerged: one which

[58] Taken from copy of report made by Herbert M. Davidson to Southern Newspaper Publishers Association.

called for a very "practical" type of training, and another which emphasized the need for broad cultural programs including a minimum of technical subjects.

Starting out in many instances as courses in English departments, the curricula which developed reflected the influence of these two philosophies. At first, the work offered generally was of a very practical nature, with major emphasis on technical skills. Gradually, the trend was toward a more equal balance between practical and cultural training, with present-day programs in leading schools of journalism stressing the importance of broad cultural background subjects as an essential part of professional curricula in journalism and in some schools the organization of five-year programs similar to those being followed by other professional schools such as law, medicine, and engineering.

With the organization of the American Association of Teachers of Journalism in 1912, and of the American Association of Schools and Departments of Journalism in 1917, attention was turned toward raising the standards of teaching, and efforts of these two organizations to improve education for journalism have been continuous. Their work, together with that of the National Council, has resulted in great improvement in the type of professional training for journalism being offered. Today, the new Revised Standards of the AASDJ are the highest of any that have preceded them, and are aimed toward producing men and women with the best possible training for entering the profession of journalism. How well the various groups of colleges and universities offering instruction in journalism measure up will be brought out in the following chapters.

CHAPTER III

GROUP A—ACCREDITED SCHOOLS OF JOURNALISM

IN CHAPTER II, the origins and development of education for journalism in this country were traced, with attention to the philosophies which grew up, the emerging curricula, and the setting of standards for the teaching of journalism. All schools which began offering instruction during this period were affected, and felt the impact of the changes which took place.

As already mentioned, the 542 schools under consideration in this study have been placed in four groups—Group A, Group B, Group C, and Group D—according to the types of programs being offered.

The purpose of this chapter will be to investigate the Group A schools, which include those accredited institutions holding membership in the American Association of Schools and Departments of Journalism. Since these are the schools which set the pattern of education for journalism in the United States, it is important that they be treated first.

The plan to be followed in this discussion of the Group A schools will include a presentation of information on the following points: origins, geographical distribution, present types of organizations, objectives, requirements for graduation, program of courses offered, enrollment, number of graduates, placement of graduates, size and preparation of staff, laboratory and library facilities, and a summary of findings. In succeeding chapters dealing with the other three groups of schools, the same general plan will be followed.

MEMBERS OF AASDJ

The thirty-two schools included in this classification are members of the American Association of Schools and Departments of Journalism—the only accrediting agency recognized within the field of education for journalism.[1] From its inception, this organization has been interested in raising the standards of schools of journalism, and the work which it has done in this direction has won the sympathetic support of leading newspaper organizations and editors throughout the country.

The "Proposed Standards for Schools of Journalism," given in Chapter II of this study, came as a result of close cooperation between the members of the AASDJ and newspapermen served by the schools of journalism.

---

[1] The admittance of Emory University in 1941 and of the University of California in 1943 to membership in the AASDJ raised the number of accredited schools to 34. However, since these schools were not members of the organization during the period covered by this survey, information concerning them will be found in Chapter 4, which deals with Group B institutions.

They are the most rigid of any previously proposed and emphasize the desire of editors and educators of journalism to improve the quality of instruction for students planning to enter the profession.

All of these institutions have fulfilled the requirements for admission to the AASDJ and thus are the only institutions entitled to professional school rating given them, when judged by the only accrediting standards considered valid by the profession. However, this does not mean that no other schools in the country are offering sound professional programs that would measure up, in most respects at least, to the requirements of this organization.

ORIGINS OF GROUP A SCHOOLS

A study of the origins of these schools of journalism indicates that professional training for journalism first took root in the Middle Western states. Although Washington and Lee University in Virginia attempted to establish the work as early as 1869, the courses were discontinued in 1878 and instruction was not attempted again there until 1925.

Kansas State College, the University of Missouri, the University of Michigan, the University of Nebraska, Ohio State University, and Indiana University all had under way before the end of the nineteenth century programs which were to develop into professional schools in the years to follow.

By 1900, eight of these Group A schools had started programs, and from 1900–10, seven more began instruction in journalism.

Before the first recognized school of journalism was organized at the University of Missouri in 1908, instruction had begun in the University of Illinois, Iowa State College, the University of Kansas, the University of Wisconsin, and the University of Oklahoma.

The period from 1908 to 1925 saw the development of instruction in journalism in the remaining institutions. Fifteen were added during the years from 1910–20; the two remaining schools in this group started with journalism in the 1920's (see Graph II).

Of significance is the fact that these earlier schools did not begin in the metropolitan areas, where the demand for trained workers was strongest. However, instruction was started in the two schools in New York City— Columbia and New York University—shortly after the opening of the school of journalism at the University of Missouri. Work at New York University commenced in 1911, and the School of Journalism at Columbia University was opened in 1912.

Stanford University, in the far West, announced its first courses in 1910, one year before the New York University program was established, and the University of Southern California made its first offerings in journalism in 1915. In the South, Texas, Louisiana, and Georgia had begun instruction by 1915.

Thus, among the schools included in Group A, concentration of population was not the controlling factor as far as early origins were concerned. Schools in the Middle Western states were the first to adopt instruction aimed toward fitting young men and women for the profession. The date of origin reported for each institution in this classification is shown in Table 2.

Contrary to the assertion sometimes heard that schools of journalism did not arise because of a need felt on the part of editors and publishers, facts

GRAPH II

GROWTH OF GROUP A SCHOOLS OF JOURNALISM

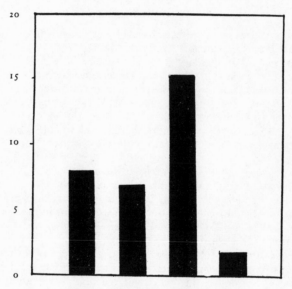

1869–1900   1900–10   1910–20   1920–25

All of the 32 Group A Schools in operation by 1940 had begun instruction by the end of 1925.

regarding the origin of many of these schools show that they were established largely through the efforts of newspapermen.

The first school of journalism—at the University of Missouri—came as a direct result of concerted efforts of the Missouri Press Association, which has cooperated closely ever since the first program of courses in journalism was offered—one which the newspapermen themselves helped shape.

The school of journalism at Columbia University in New York—second to be founded in this country—was created at the behest of, and through a large endowment by, Joseph Pulitzer, a metropolitan newspaper publisher and one of the greatest journalists this country ever produced.

At Rutgers University, the department of journalism was brought into existence through the initiative of the New Jersey Press Association, which has cooperated in sponsoring and developing the program. The school at Washington and Lee University likewise was made possible by funds subscribed by members of the Southern Newspaper Publishers Association.

TABLE 2

DATES OF ORIGIN OF INSTRUCTION IN JOURNALISM
FOR ALL GROUP A SCHOOLS

State	School	Date Instruction Started
California	Stanford University	1910
	Univ. of So. California	1915
Colorado	Univ. of Colorado	1909
Georgia	Univ. of Georgia	1915
Illinois	Northwestern University	1921
	Univ. of Illinois	1902
Indiana	Indiana University	1893
Iowa	Iowa State College	1905
	State Univ. of Iowa	1892
Kansas	Kansas State College	1873
	University of Kansas	1903
Kentucky	University of Kentucky	1914
Louisiana	Louisiana State Univ.	1912
Massachusetts	Boston University	1914
Michigan	University of Michigan	1895
Minnesota	University of Minnesota	1910
Missouri	University of Missouri	1878
Montana	Montana State University	1914
Nebraska	University of Nebraska	1894
New Jersey	Rutgers University	1925
New York	Columbia University	1912
	New York University	1911
	Syracuse University	1919
Ohio	Ohio State University	1895
Oklahoma	University of Oklahoma	1908
Oregon	University of Oregon	1912
Pennsylvania	Pennsylvania State College	1914
Texas	University of Texas	1914
Virginia	Washington and Lee University	1869–78; 1925
Washington	University of Washington	1909
Wisconsin	Marquette University	1910
	University of Wisconsin	1905

The Medill School of Journalism at Northwestern University came into being as a result of an endowment by the owners of the *Chicago Tribune*, and it bears the name of Joseph Medill, famous editor of that paper. The *Tribune* has continued to assist the school financially during the years that have followed.

The School of Journalism at the University of Minnesota was endowed through the will of William J. Murphy, former publisher of the *Minneapolis Tribune*.

In an effort to expand the benefits of professional training in journalism abroad, a group of leading publishers and editors in the United States created a fund of $70,000, in 1928, for the creation of the first school of journalism in China, under the auspices of the Missouri-Yenching Foundation.[2]

By 1938, twelve state press associations had formed connections with schools of journalism by providing for the secretary of each to serve also as a part-time member of the faculty of the journalism school in his particular area. This plan at that time was being followed by Colorado, Georgia, Idaho, Illinois, Louisiana, Michigan, Missouri, New Jersey, New York, Oregon, Washington, and Wisconsin.[3]

Other examples might be cited to show the strong cooperation which this journalism-education movement has received from interested newspapermen and state and regional newspaper organizations the country over. In many cases, editors and publishers are taking an active part in providing instruction by giving lectures, by making their newspaper plants available for laboratory purposes, or by assisting in other ways.

Not all of the accredited schools of journalism in the beginning were sponsored by newspapermen. Some of them, like those at the Universities of Wisconsin, Oklahoma, and Kansas, grew out of English departments as a result of student demand for training in journalism. However, all of them, regardless of the forces which brought them into being, have reached their level of development largely through the support they have received from newspapermen as well as educators, and today they are highly respected by members of the profession which they serve.

GEOGRAPHICAL DISTRIBUTION

These 32 schools and departments of journalism are distributed through 25 states, leaving a total of 23 states not represented. New York has three Group A schools; California, Illinois, Iowa, Kansas, and Wisconsin have two each. Each of the remaining 19 states is served by one school classified in this group.

As may be seen by the map on page 108 showing the geographical distribution, the states in the far West and in the South are served by fewer Group A schools of journalism than are the other sections of the United States. Greatest concentration is in the Middle Western states, where the first courses in journalism were introduced.

[2] Nash, *Educating for Journalism*, p. 28.
[3] *Ibid.*, p. 33.

PRESENT TYPES OF ORGANIZATIONS

All of these 32 professional schools of journalism are in recognized institutions of higher learning. Twenty-three are in state universities and nine are in privately endowed universities.

The general enrollments of the universities represented range in size from 934 at Washington and Lee University to 30,408 at New York University.

Nine of the professional schools are autonomous, responsible only to the president of the university on the same basis as schools of law and medicine; nine are independent schools in the colleges of liberal arts; two are departments in schools of commerce; two are departments in schools of agriculture or science; and one is a department in the school of social science.

The School of Journalism at Columbia University is strictly a graduate school, requiring the baccalaureate degree for admittance. All the rest accept students of undergraduate status, but the level of admission is not uniform, as may be seen by the following analysis:

No. Schools	Level of Admission
3	Freshman
2	Sophomore
25	Junior
1	Senior
1	Graduate

Although admission to the professional school is delayed in 26 of the institutions until the junior year, all except Columbia University and the University of Missouri offer introductory courses dealing with the history of journalism or a survey of the field of journalism before the beginning of the third year. Records made by students in these early courses serve as one of the determining factors regulating admission to the professional programs.

In every instance, those admitted to the professional school must present satisfactory records in work done up to that point, with an average of "C" or better in the courses already undertaken. The Medill School of Journalism, following the five-year plan, requires a "B" average in the first three years of university work.

Other special requirements include the following: (1) satisfactory scores in vocational and aptitude tests in two schools; (2) passing of proficiency test in typewriting, two schools; (3) satisfactory grades in proficiency examinations in English, two schools; (4) passing of proficiency test in one language, one school; (5) satisfactory interviews with faculty or newspaper representatives before making the final decision, two schools; and (6) passing of physical examination, one school.

All of these requirements, which vary somewhat from school to school, are set up for the common purpose of assisting in the selection of only those students who show promise of success in the profession of journalism. As a result, many of the unfit are weeded out, and in most of these schools only about 50 per-cent of the pre-journalism freshmen are finally admitted to the journalism program. In this way, the Group A schools undoubtedly are doing the profession a service by training only those men and women possessing the qualifications considered essential for the highest type of newspaper work.

TABLE 3

LEVEL OF ADMISSION IN GROUP A SCHOOLS

School	Year Admitted
Stanford University	Junior
University of Southern California	Junior
University of Colorado	Junior
University of Georgia	Junior
Northwestern University	Senior
University of Illinois	Junior
Indiana University	Junior
Iowa State College	Junior
State University of Iowa	Junior
Kansas State College	Sophomore
University of Kansas	Junior
University of Kentucky	Junior
Louisiana State University	Junior
Boston University	Freshman
University of Michigan	Junior
University of Minnesota	Junior
University of Missouri	Junior
Montana State University	Junior
University of Nebraska	Freshman
Rutgers University	Junior
Columbia University	Graduate
New York University	Junior
Syracuse University	Junior
Ohio State University	Junior
University of Oklahoma	Sophomore
University of Oregon	Junior
Pennsylvania State College	Junior
University of Texas	Junior
Washington and Lee University	Junior
University of Washington	Junior
Marquette University	Freshman
University of Wisconsin	Junior

OBJECTIVES

These schools have definite professional objectives. All of them aim to train students for positions on newspapers or in allied journalistic fields. In order to accomplish this end, the instruction is designed (1) to give a thorough liberal background with emphasis on the social sciences and (2) to provide sound professional training for journalistic work, including not only an understanding of principles and techniques, but also an appreciation of the press as a social institution that places wide responsibilities on those engaged in the work.

Commenting upon the philosophy of education in journalism, Dean Carl W. Ackerman, of the School of Journalism, Columbia University, helps clarify the demands of the profession and the needs that schools of journalism must attempt to fill in training students. He says:

The profession of journalism today makes exacting demands on its personnel. It demands an increasing accuracy of knowledge. Editors and reporters must be able and willing to adapt themselves to organized discipline without losing their individuality. They must have the ability to obtain accurate information and the industry to interpret and report it within constantly shrinking periods of time. They must have the capacity to pursue a continuous process of education. They must have the ability to comprehend the developments in any specialized field of human action. They must develop an international viewpoint without losing a domestic conciousness; and above all they must have an idealism and a balance which can not only withstand the stress of experience but aid in strengthening the idealism of a profession which is repeatedly shaken by the intimate contact with the weaknesses and the failures of human institutions.

Under these conditions we must place a high value upon our responsibilities to the profession if we wish to expect our graduates to value highly their responsibilities.

It is self-evident in journalism, as well as in education, that there is a gap between knowing something and making that something of value to someone else. Knowledge, obviously, is of value only when it is used. The education of a writer or editor must not only be continuous but it must be used continuously to have value. The more it is used the greater its social and economic value because the primary function of this profession is to collect, interpret, and distribute facts and ideas for the information of a discriminating reading public.

As journalism is becoming more and more of a public service, our function must be to prepare men and women to assume increasing responsibilities, to discharge faithfully their larger responsibilities to society and "to think in terms of tomorrow, to feel in terms of new human relationships" . . . [4]

Here the emphasis is placed upon the acquisition of a wide background of knowledge and the development of social consciousness. The attempts of the Group A schools of journalism to strive for these objectives is reflected in courses of study heavily weighted on the side of the social sciences.

REQUIREMENTS FOR GRADUATION

All 32 schools in this group grant degrees or provide majors in journalism. A study of requirements for graduation reveals that an average of 23.3 per-cent of the four- and five-year programs is devoted to journalism courses, leaving 76.7 per-cent of the student's time for background courses.

The average number of semester credits required for the bachelor's de-

[4] *Catalog* (Graduate School of Journalism, Columbia University, 1939-40), p. 8.

gree ranges from 120 to 136 hours. Out of this total, an average of 29.1 semester hours must be in journalism courses. Columbia University and Northwestern University, which offer only the master's degree, require 146 and 150 hours respectively for graduation.

PROGRAM OF COURSES OFFERED

The finding that 76.7 per-cent of the student's time is spent outside the school of journalism in acquiring background and cultural information is particularly interesting in that it tends to dispel any doubts regarding an answer to the charge sometimes heard that an individual training for journalism spends practically all of his time studying nothing but journalism—which many outsiders still think consists mainly of reporting, copy editing, and other technical subjects.

On the contrary, less than 24 per-cent of the journalism graduate's time is occupied with the curriculum of the professional school; and, furthermore, as will be shown later, 17.6 per-cent of the courses offered by these 32 schools deals with courses aimed definitely at providing further background, as well as an interpretation and understanding of the close relationship between the information gained through studies pursued outside the professional school and the work provided within the curriculum of journalism itself.

Such a plan is in keeping with the modern educational view that much of a student's time in college should be spent in obtaining a liberal education. Dean Kenneth E. Olson, of the Medill School of Journalism, Northwestern University, in his presidential address before the 1938 convention of the American Association of Schools and Departments of Journalism, pointed out the advantages of placing more emphasis on broadening the general education base for students of journalism. Commenting on the announcements of five-year plans of education for journalism, adopted some time before by Stanford, Iowa, and Northwestern, he had this to say:

I hold no brief for any of these plans—certainly we do not feel that our plan at Northwestern is necessarily the final answer—but we do think it is a step in the right direction. It does make for a substantial gain in the amount of liberal education required and a gain as well in the professional development possible when students with a broader education undertake professional studies. It does enable us to give our students a better foundation in economics, history, political science, sociology and the integration of these studies and journalism. It does bring us closer to that ideal of a graduate professional school on the same level as schools of law and medicine which the Society of Newspaper Editors commended as our ultimate goal back in 1925.[5]

Under the five-year plan being offered at Northwestern University, the student must meet all of the liberal arts requirements for a first degree, including a field of concentration in one of the social sciences or English.

[5] Olson, "Schools of Journalism and the Press," *Journalism Quarterly*, XVI, (1939), p. 35.

In the estimation of Dean Olson, the schools of journalism, aided by news-papermen, probably have made as much progress in this direction as schools of law and medicine, and will have fewer problems to overcome in further readjusting their curriculum to meet present-day needs. He stated his views in this regard as follows:

In attacking our problem our major newspaper organizations will not have as far to go as did the medical and legal associations. When they started to clean up their schools, they merely concentrated on technical courses. All they did about cultural education was to demand, progressively, first a high school education, then one year of college, later two years of college and now three years of college. Even at present, in the case of medical schools, much of these three years is devoted to material that is vocationally narrow. It is only now that doctors and lawyers are beginning to discover that they have attacked only half of the problem. I am not sure but that in some respects we are as far along toward the final answer as are the schools of law and medicine; for we have to the best of our ability been insisting upon a cultural and social ingredient in our education and have devoted ourselves largely to the ap-plication of social sciences to the field of public affairs. At Northwestern our school is organized on the same basis as the law school. Just as does our law school, we re-quire three years of college work for admission. Just as do law students, our stu-dents carry a joint-degree program with the college of liberal arts and receive their first degree from this college. Just as does the law school, we grant only the profes-sional degree on the completion of a professional program superimposed on a liberal education. We differ from the law school in that our program is not so profession-ally narrow but provides opportunity for advanced work in social sciences.[6]

Speaking before The American Society of Newspaper Editors during their annual convention in 1938, where he called upon these newspapermen to cooperate with the schools of journalism in their efforts to raise the standards of education for journalism, Dean Olson again pointed out the trend toward a broader general education for students seeking training for the profession, and emphasized this fact:

What these schools (of journalism) are trying to do is to provide a special educa-tional program that cuts around the usual college restrictions and enables the student to get the rich background in history, economics, politics and literature which ordi-nary liberal arts graduates do not get.[7]

An analysis of course-offerings of the 32 accredited AASDJ schools shows that all of them offer some background courses. All give a high per-centage of courses on the news side; 30 offer courses dealing with business problems; 28 give courses in allied fields, such as radio, magazine-writing, short-story writing, teaching of journalism, and public relations; and 31 have offerings in the graphic arts, including typography, photography, and engraving.

[6] Ibid., 35–6.
[7] Problems of Journalism (Washington, D. C.: Proceedings of the Sixteenth Annual Convention of The American Society of Newspaper Editors, 1938), p. 46.

In the computation of the number of courses offered by a school, each listing in the catalog was not considered as one. In the case of two courses, for instance, where the second was a continuation of the first one listed, both were considered as only one course. Thus, News Reporting I and News Reporting II (a continuation of the work in News Reporting I) were regarded as a single course. The name of a course and the description of its content were used in determining its classification. Courses dealing with social, ethical, historical and other related cultural material were listed as "background." Included in this grouping were such courses as the following:

American Journalists
Comparative Journalism
Contemporary Affairs
Contemporary Newspapers
Contemporary Thought
Correlation of Journalism (with other subjects)
Current Events
Early Development of the Press
Ethics of Journalism
Foreign News and the European Press
Geographical Aspects of Journalism
History of Freedom of the Press
History of Journalism
Influence of the Newspaper
Journalism and Society
Journalism for Women
Journalism Vocations
Literature of Journalism
Literary Aspects of Journalism
Newspaper Crusades
Newspaper Problems and Policies
Press Systems of the World
Propaganda and Censorship
Public Opinion
Social Influence of the Press
Sociological Aspects of Journalism
Survey of Journalism
Techniques in Propaganda
The American Newspaper
The European Background
The Press and World Affairs
The Press as a Social Instrument

All courses concerned with the writing and handling of news were classified under the heading of "news." Those dealing with reporting, news writing, feature writing, the editorial, copyreading and news editing were among the subjects falling into this grouping.

"Business" courses were those that had to do with the business aspects of newspaper-publishing, including advertising, circulation, newspaper-management, and the like.

"Allied" courses were regarded as those offering information in fields closely related to the newspaper, such as radio, magazine and short-story writing, and technical journalism.

Under "graphic arts" were listed subjects having to do with a study of typography, newspaper mechanics and makeup, printing, photography and engraving.

This method of classification revealed that a total of 789 courses were being offered by the 32 schools under consideration. They were distributed as follows:

Type of Course	Number	% of Total
Background	139	17.6
News	380	48.1
Business	136	17.3
Allied	75	9.5
Graphic Arts	59	7.5
Total	789	100.0

Of significance was the finding that more background courses than business courses were offered by these 32 schools. Furthermore, contrary to the assumption by many newspapermen that most of a student's time is consumed in learning how to write news stories, edit copy, and perform other "practical" newsroom tasks, less than 50 per-cent of the courses in these schools deal directly with this aspect of the work.

Breakdowns for individual schools would show even a smaller percentage of "news" and "business" courses, in some instances, than is indicated by the figures above.

The average number of courses offered by these schools was 23.4. The highest number offered was 50; the lowest, 12. Total semester-hours of work offered in courses in journalism varied from 28 to 150, with an average of 62 hours for the entire group.

These findings indicated that a typical program of 23.4 courses for the average school would include the following:

Background Courses	4.5
News Courses	9.2
Business Courses	4.2
Allied Courses	3.5
Graphic Arts Courses	2.0
	23.4

ENROLLMENT

During the year 1939–40, these schools had a total enrollment of 6,390 students, or an average of 196 for each school. The highest number reported by any one school was 395 (the University of Missouri), which figure included only students enrolled in the professional school. The lowest was 66 (Washington and Lee University).

It should be pointed out that although these 32 schools reported 6,390 students enrolled in programs of journalism, only about half of this number was registered in the professional schools themselves. The rest were in colleges of liberal arts following pre-journalism programs, in preparation for entrance into the professional journalism programs in the junior year or later.

Out of the total number of 6,390 students reported, 3,038 were enrolled in pre-journalism courses. With the exception of one school (Northwestern

TABLE 4

NUMBER OF GRADUATES FROM GROUP A SCHOOLS
OVER THREE-YEAR PERIOD*

Year	Bachelors	Masters	J.D.	Total
1937	1,087	102	1	1,190
1938	1,269	103	0	1,372
1939	1,224	128	0	1,352
Total........	3,580	333	1	3,914

* (For complete breakdown by schools, see Appendix B.)

University), where juniors are regarded as pre-journalism, these pre-journalism students were freshmen and sophomores.

Professional enrollment, consisting of juniors, seniors, and graduate students, amounted to 3,352, or 53.2 per-cent of the total. The highest number of professional students reported by any one school was 395; the lowest, 25. Average professional enrollment was 104 students per school.

NUMBER OF GRADUATES

Reports from these 32 schools show that, in 1939, degrees were granted to 1,352 students. Of this total, 128 were master's. Figures for 1938 indicate that 1,372 received degrees; and in 1937, 1,190.

This represents a total output of approximately 41 graduates annually for each of the schools of journalism in this group, or about 1,300 a year for all 32 combined. Almost ten per-cent of these graduates each year receive the master's degree, and the proportion of the higher degree has increased steadily over the three-year period from 1937 to 1939, inclusive.

Only one institution—the University of Missouri—grants the doctor's degree in journalism. However, in some of the other schools—including Northwestern, Wisconsin, and Minnesota—journalism may serve as a minor for the doctor of philosophy degree. Not included in the above figures was the granting of two such degrees at the University of Wisconsin in 1937.

An increase in the number of master's degrees, from 102 in 1937 to 128 in 1939, indicates a probable trend toward greater emphasis on graduate work as preparation for the profession.

Although there was an increase of 182 degrees in 1938 over the previous year, the number granted in 1939 was 20 less than in 1938, but still 162 above 1937.

Washington and Lee University, which reported the granting of only 23 degrees over the three-year period, was the lowest in the group; the highest number of degrees granted over the same period by any one institution was 554 by the University of Missouri.

PLACEMENT OF GRADUATES

Thirty of the 32 schools reporting on placements for the year 1939 showed that almost 70 per-cent of the graduates were absorbed by the profession of journalism. (See Appendix C.)

Out of a total of 862 finding positions, 568—almost 65 per-cent—were placed on newspapers; 294, or 35 per-cent, were employed in allied fields.

The fact that the remaining 374 graduates in 1939 did not find newspaper positions should not be regarded, however, as an unfavorable reflection upon the ability of these schools to find positions for students who receive degrees. Previous studies on the placement of graduates from some of these institutions have shown that approximately 15 per-cent enter business or related journalistic fields; around 3 per-cent continue their studies in graduate schools or in other professional schools, such as law; and many of the women graduates are married soon after graduation or follow some pursuit other than journalism.

Statements from deans and department-heads of the Group A schools also indicated that practically every graduate who wanted a journalistic position succeeded in finding one. Furthermore, several schools reported 100 per-cent placement except for the depression years of 1932, 1933, and 1937. In normal years, the demand for journalism graduates appears to have far exceeded the supply.

Some schools reported that complete records on placement were not kept, and gave estimates; two schools failed to report. Consequently, the percentage of placements may have been higher than available figures indicate.

In order to get a broad view of the distribution of placements, the schools were asked to estimate the average number of students placed in the various fields for each year over the last five years. Although these five years included a period of depression during which business dropped sharply, with its consequent effects on employment in the newspaper profession, these findings serve to stress the importance which publishers placed on the necessity of securing well-trained workers and the manner in which professional schools of journalism helped fill that need. Answers from 31 schools gave the following results:

Type of work	No. Placed	% of Total
Daily Newspapers	332.60	39.75
Weekly Newspapers	114.80	13.80
Press Associations	40.88	4.95
Syndicates	8.01	.95
Business Publications	34.31	4.20
Magazines	41.47	4.90
Radio Work	42.00	5.00
Publicity	50.15	6.00
Advertising (other than newspaper)	126.39	15.00
Other Types (Teaching, etc.)	45.40	5.45
Total	836.00	100.00

An average of 332.6 graduates, over the five-year period—or almost 40 per-cent—were placed on daily newspapers. A further breakdown reveals that of this number, 244 entered the news side. Placed in advertising were 82.3; and 10.7 were engaged in circulation work. This represents a total of 93 graduates, or 27.9 per-cent of those entering the daily field, who started their journalistic careers on the business side.

Add to these 93 the 126 who were placed in advertising, other than newspaper, and 114.8 graduates who found jobs on weekly newspapers, where a knowledge of both the business and editorial phases of newspaper publishing is essential, and it is found that a total of slightly more than 344 graduates, or approximately 41 per-cent of the total number of 836 placed in all lines, entered business fields. Of equal significance is the fact that this total of 344 graduates entering the business side (including weeklies) is greater by 19.4 than the 332.6 who found jobs in the news departments of daily newspapers. These findings would seem to emphasize the necessity of placing more stress on "business" courses in the curriculum in journalism.

Until recent years, schools of journalism paid little attention to this type of instruction in their curricula. However, findings concerning course-offerings, mentioned earlier in this chapter, show that 17.3 per-cent of the courses in the average journalism program at the time of this study were devoted to "business," as compared to 48.1 per-cent dealing with "news." Likewise, since 40 per-cent of all the graduates placed went into daily newspapers and another 13.8 per-cent was absorbed by weekly newspapers —representing 53.8 per-cent of the total placements—the apparent conclusion to be drawn is that major emphasis should be given to preparing students for work on these two types of publications, with a much smaller degree of attention being devoted to training in other related fields. Reports on course-offerings indicate that this is being done; however, as pointed out, more emphasis appears to be needed on "business" courses in this preparation.

SIZE OF TEACHING STAFF

A total of 258 staff-members were found to be engaged in teaching journalism in the 32 schools during 1939-40, making an average of eight teachers for each. However, one school reported only three men on the staff; the largest number on any one staff was 19.

TABLE 5

STAFF DISTRIBUTION ACCORDING TO SIZE
IN THE GROUP A SCHOOLS

No. Schools	Size of Staff
1	3
2	4
4	5
9	6
2	7
2	8
2	9
3	10
1	11
2	12
2	13
1	15
1	19
32	258

In addition to the number of regular staff-members, every school in this group makes a practice of inviting newspapermen and representatives from other related journalistic fields for lectures during the school year. Thus, the work given by the staff-members is supplemented in every case by instruction given by men engaged in journalism.

On the other hand, many of the regular staff-members have other duties besides teaching journalism. Reports from all of the schools indicate that 96 staff-members out of the total of 258 are engaged in other types of work in connection with their journalism teaching. Fifty-two are working newspapermen, devoting part time to teaching journalism; seventeen do part of their teaching in other fields within their respective universities; and ten spend from one-third to three-fourths of their time with the University Press. This leaves 162 staff-members devoting full time to the teaching of journalism. By further deduction of fractions of time reported by part-time instructors as spent on other duties, the average full-time staff in these 32 schools was found to be 4.7 persons.

Every school had the equivalent of three or more full-time staff members. The largest full time staff reported consisted of 13 members. Distribution of full time staff members in the 32 schools was as follows:

No. Schools	No. Full Time Members (or equivalent)
10	3
5	4
5	5
7	6
3	7
1	10
1	13

ACADEMIC RANK OF STAFF MEMBERS

A classification of these 258 staff-members according to academic rank shows that the largest number, or 24.81 per-cent, are full professors. Next in point of number are assistant professors, with 23.26 per-cent.

Associate professors make up 13.56 per-cent; instructors, 15.89; lecturers, 15.5; and assistants, 6.98 per-cent. The complete distribution is shown below:

Rank	No.	% of Total
Professor.....................	64	24.81
Associate Professor..............	35	13.56
Assistant Professor..............	60	23.26
Instructor.....................	41	15.89
Lecturer......................	40	15.50
Assistant.....................	18	6.98
Total.....................	258	100.00

PREPARATION OF STAFF MEMBERS

In order to determine the preparation of staff-members, their records were investigated from three points of view: academic preparation, teaching experience, and journalistic experience, including work done on newspapers or in allied fields.

The largest number of staff members—45.35 per-cent—was found to hold master's degrees; 36.44 per-cent had bachelor's; and only 13.56 per-cent of the total had doctor's degrees. Twelve staff members in the 32 schools, or 4.65 per-cent, had no college degrees; however, most of these are seasoned newspapermen with many years of experience. For instance, one staff member not holding a degree was reported as having spent 30 years as city editor on a leading metropolitan daily newspaper, and consequently is highly valuable to the school in which he is teaching.

Eleven schools had no men with Ph.D. degrees, and the school with the highest number reported four.

Average teaching experience for the various schools in this classification ranged from a low of 5.3 years to a high of 19. The average for all 258 staff members was 11.3 years.

A wide variation also was apparent in the amount of journalistic experience listed for teachers in the 31 schools reporting. Computations for the
group as a whole resulted in the finding of an average of 7.2 years of newspaper experience for each staff member, and the average allied journalistic
experience in such fields as advertising, magazine work, business publication, radio and so forth, figured in the same manner, amounted to 3.7. Thus,
on this basis, the total average journalistic experience for each staff member
in these schools was 10.9 years.

However, some staff members in these schools were found to have had
very little newspaper experience. On the other hand, many of the men have

TABLE 6

ACADEMIC PERPARATION OF STAFF MEMBERS
IN AASDJ SCHOOLS

No. Staff Members	Degrees Held	Per-cent of Total
31	Ph.D.	12.01
4	J.D.	1.55
117	M.A. or M.S.	45.35
94	B.A. or B.S.	36.44
12	No Degree	4.65
258		100.00

had from 15 to as high as 30 years of actual newspaper experience, and a
majority of those listed had more than seven years. This situation undoubtedly is largely a result of the requirement set up in 1928 by the American Association of Schools and Departments of Journalism which provided
that staff members in these schools should have a minimum of five years of
newspaper experience. At any rate, it indicates that member schools have
made an honest attempt to follow this policy, and that the teaching of
journalism is attracting an increasing number of experienced newspapermen
to staffs of the Group A schools.

In the computation of journalistic experience, only that time actually
spent as full time members of newspaper staffs—or in allied fields—was considered as an accurate measuring device. Time spent as correspondents for
press associations or newspapers, while carrying on teaching or other duties,
was credited as one-third of actual full-time employment. Experience on
school newspapers, magazines or yearbooks and work as supervisors of such
publications was not counted.

The three schools indicating the largest amount of journalistic experience
for their entire staffs showed an average of 15–19 years. Four years was
reported by the two schools with the lowest average.

TABLE 7

AVERAGE JOURNALISTIC EXPERIENCE OF STAFFS
IN AASDJ SCHOOLS

No. Schools	Av. Yrs. Experience
2	4– 4½
7	5– 6
5	6– 7
4	7– 8
3	8–10
3	10–12
4	12–15
3	15–19
31	

LABORATORY AND LIBRARY FACILITIES

All 32 schools provide completely-equipped city rooms, reporting and news editing laboratories, where students may get practice in writing and handling news under conditions closely duplicating those of actual newspaper offices. In every school, those in charge of these laboratories have had experience in the fields represented. Twelve institutions provide direct wire services.

In addition to the news facilities, laboratories for advertising, typography, engraving and radio are provided in several of the schools. Eleven have well-equipped newspaper plants, and seventeen have standing arrangements with coöperating daily or weekly newspapers whereby students may gain first-hand experience. Eleven schools either publish or assist with the publication of school papers. Distribution of laboratory facilities by kinds was as follows:

No. Schools	Laboratory Provided
12	Wire Services
11	Advertising
26	Typography
18	Photography
8	Engraving
11	Radio
11	Newspaper Plants
17	Cooperating Newspapers
11	School Papers

All 32 schools have their own newspaper reading-rooms and departmental libraries, supplemented by collections of books on journalism in the regular university libraries.

The absence of advertising laboratories in 21 schools indicates either that less emphasis is given to this phase of training in journalism or that the facilities are inadequate for carrying on such work in a high percentage of the institutions. A study of the kinds of courses offered, given earlier in this chapter, lends support to the former of these two assumptions.

Provision for typography laboratories in 26 of the 32 schools emphasizes the importance placed on an understanding of types and their use. Inclusion of photography, engraving and radio laboratories in some of the schools also shows a tendency to branch out into departments of newspaper publication and allied fields that have gained considerable impetus in the last few years.

SUMMARY

The 32 Group A schools considered in this chapter are carrying on professional programs definitely designed to train students for work on newspapers or in allied journalistic fields. Organized as separate units granting degrees or majors, all of them are recognized by their respective institutions as integral parts of higher education.

The curriculum is so arranged that approximately one-fourth of the student's time is devoted to courses given in the professional schools of journalism. A wide cultural background in the social sciences, supplemented by practical training, is considered necessary. Furthermore, entrance is delayed in most of the schools until the third year. The facts that one school does not admit students until they are seniors, and another is strictly a graduate school, lead to the assumption that the tendency is toward an increasing emphasis upon a broad background before entering the professional program which places some stress upon techniques as well as upon the cultural, ethical and social aspects of journalism.

The absorption of graduates of these 32 schools by the profession is high. As pointed out earlier in this chapter, approximately 70 per-cent of those receiving degrees in 1939 found positions. In some schools, the percentage receiving employment was considerably higher. Columbia University, Northwestern University, and several other schools reported 100 per-cent placement of all graduates available for jobs upon graduation. Practically every graduate of these schools who wants a journalistic position is placed.

This situation is, indeed, a high tribute on the part of the profession to these schools of journalism and reflects the faith that newspapers today are placing in colleges and universities as a reliable source of supply from which they can draw recruits that measure up to ever-stiffening requirements. It also undoubtedly accounts for their increasing interest and cooperation in attempts to raise the level of journalistic training, which in turn will benefit the newspapers and the society which they serve.

Staffs in these 32 schools appear to be well prepared to provide effective educational programs in journalism. Their academic training and teaching experience, bolstered by several years of actual work in journalistic fields, should fit them for training students who would be acceptable by the profession.

Likewise, laboratory and library facilities are provided, thus giving an

opportunity for practical application of principles and techniques in situations typical of those that will be met upon employment.

Definite efforts are being made in these schools to lay the groundwork for
participation of their graduates in the profession of journalism by means of
a functional program under conditions that encourage, and make possible,
the testing of theory by actual practice, under the guidance of highly-trained
staff members.

In the following chapter, other schools and departments of journalism
not members of the American Association of Schools and Departments of
Journalism will be considered. Programs offered in these schools follow
closely the pattern established by the Group A institutions, but as a whole
the Group B offerings are not so strong, and fail to meet the requirements
set up by the AASDJ for membership.

CHAPTER IV

GROUP B—OTHER SCHOOLS AND DEPART-
MENTS OF JOURNALISM

IN ADDITION to the thirty-two schools considered in Chapter III, seventy-one other institutions in the United States were found to be offering substantial programs of journalism leading to degrees or majors. (See Table 8). Of this number, sixty-eight are universities and colleges, and three are teachers' colleges.

Undoubtedly, it is possible for as few as two men on a staff to teach a group of fifteen or twenty students effectively if provided ample laboratory and library facilities—as is the case in several of the schools in Group B—but so small a staff, in itself, would bar it from acceptance by the AASDJ, whose proposed standards for education for journalism call for a minimum staff of three members holding professorial rank.

This does not mean that some of these smaller schools are not meeting the needs of their more limited areas very successfully, and a few, as already pointed out, are offering sound programs that could meet—at least in some respects—the requirements set up for schools holding membership in the AASDJ.

The purpose of this chapter will be to analyze the work being offered by these seventy-one institutions, and from these findings to draw some conclusions regarding their preparation for carrying on professional training, as compared with the schools now holding membership in the AASDJ.

ORIGINS AND DISTRIBUTION

Instruction in journalism did not begin in any of the Group B schools until after the establishment of the first professional program at the University of Missouri in 1908. In fact, the first attempt to begin work in the subject in any of the schools in this group was not made until 1912, and only 10 had started programs of journalism by 1920 (see Graph III).

The greatest period of expansion came between the years 1920–30, which saw the rise of instruction in journalism in 38 of the institutions. Reports from 56 of the 71 schools reveal that eight of these schools have started courses since then. Most of the 15 schools not giving information on this point indicated that the dates on which instruction began were not known.

Emory University (Georgia),[1] the University of Notre Dame (Indiana), Grinnell College (Iowa), and Trinity University (Texas) were the first

---

[1] As mentioned previously, Emory University was admitted to the American Association of Schools and Departments of Journalism in December, 1941.

TABLE 8

GROUP B SCHOOLS OF JOURNALISM AND DATES
OF ORIGIN OF INSTRUCTION

State	School	Date Instruction Started
Alabama	Univ. of Alabama	1926
Arkansas	Harding College	1924
	Univ. of Arkansas	1919
California	Col. of the Holy Name (not ac.)	—
	Fresno State College	1928
	San Francisco State College	—
	San Jose State College	1934
	University of California	1926
	Woodbury College	—
Colorado	Denver University	1920
	Loretto Heights College	1925
	Register College of Journalism	—
Florida	Florida Southern College	—
	Florida State College for Women	1928
	University of Florida	1916
	University of Tampa	—
Georgia	Emory University	1912
	Mercer University	—
Idaho	University of Idaho	1915
Indiana	Butler University	1925
	Saint Mary-of-the-Woods College	1926
	University of Notre Dame	1912
Iowa	Coe College	1913
	Drake University	1919
	Grinnell College	1912
Kansas	Baker University	—
	University of Wichita	1927
Louisiana	Louisiana Polytechnic Institute	1929
	Loyola University of the South	1934
	Tulane University	1926
Maryland	University of Baltimore	—
Massachusetts	Suffolk University	1936
Michigan	Marygrove College	1920
	Michigan State College	1921
	University of Detroit	—
Missouri	Washington University	1931
Nebraska	Creighton University	1926
	Hastings College	1934
	Midland College	1928
Nevada	University of Nevada	1922
New Jersey	Rider College (not accredited)	1930
North Carolina	University of North Carolina	1922
North Dakota	University of North Dakota	1922
Ohio	Kent State University	1937
	Ohio University	1924

TABLE 8—(Continued)

GROUP B SCHOOLS OF JOURNALISM AND DATES OF
ORIGIN OF INSTRUCTION

State	School	Date Instruction Started
	Western Reserve University, Cleveland College	1924
Oklahoma	Oklahoma A. and M. College	1922
	Oklahoma Baptist University	—
	Oklahoma City University	—
Pennsylvania	Lehigh University	1927
	College Misericordia	1938
	St. Joseph's College	—
	Temple University	1922
	University of Scranton	1926
South Carolina	University of South Carolina	1923
South Dakota	South Dakota State College	1925
	University of South Dakota	1915
Texas	Baylor University	1925
	Hardin-Simmons University	—
	Mary Hardin-Baylor University	1923
	Southern Methodist University	1920
	Texas Christian University	1927
	Texas State College for Women	1925
	Texas Technological College	1926
	Trinity University	1912
Utah	Brigham Young University	1922
West Virginia	Bethany College	1932
	Marshall College	1923
	West Virginia University	1920
Wisconsin	Mount Mary College	—
Wyoming	University of Wyoming	1926

institutions in this group to begin courses in journalism, all of them giving their initial work in 1912.

Before 1920, the University of South Dakota, Drake University (Iowa), Coe College (Iowa), the University of Idaho, the University of Florida, and the University of Arkansas had started instruction in journalism.

In these schools—just as was true with members of the AASDJ—the establishment of education for journalism apparently was not influenced by density of population, in centers where the need for trained workers was strongest, but it had its origin in the Middle Western and Southern states. Furthermore, most of the schools in Group B are in the Middle Western states. The greatest concentration occurs in Texas, which contains eight, and has in addition one school of journalism holding membership in the AASDJ, making a total of nine.

These nine schools, all of them expressing definite professional objectives, are serving a state with a population of 6,414,824 people and one which has a total of 784 daily and weekly newspapers. However, by contrast, the state of Illinois, with a population of 7,874,155 people and 868

GRAPH III

GROWTH OF GROUP B SCHOOLS OF JOURNALISM

(Based on Reports from 56 of These Institutions)

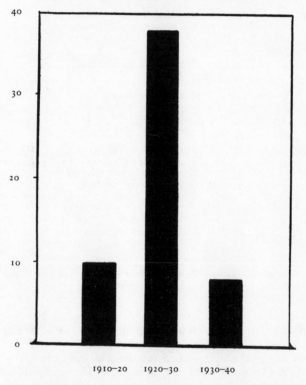

daily and weekly newspapers (see Appendix D) has only two member schools of the AASDJ and no institutions represented in Group B.

In the East, Pennsylvania, having a population smaller by over three and one-half million and containing 197 less daily and weekly newspapers than the adjoining state of New York, is being served by five Group B schools and one Group A school. New York has only three AASDJ schools and none of the Group B classification.

On the west coast, California, with over a million less population and 111 fewer newspapers than Illinois, has two AASDJ schools and six Group B institutions. Other similar situations existing in the United States might be pointed out.

Thus, the number of schools in the various states represented does not correlate with the size of population, and the number of newspapers apparently has had no important regulatory effect on the origin of professional programs in certain areas. Furthermore, it would appear that some of these states are over-supplied, when judged in terms of the number of schools as compared to size of population and the number of newspapers served.

On the other hand, ten states in this country have no schools represented in Group A and Group B. They are Arizona and New Mexico in the Southwest; Mississippi in the deep South; Tennessee and Delaware in the Middle East; and Connecticut, Rhode Island, Vermont, New Hampshire and Maine in conservative New England.

Probably the sparsely-settled states of Arizona and New Mexico, each with a population of around one-half million and together containing only 131 daily and weekly newspapers, feel that they are being served adequately by the 23 schools in the states of California, Nevada, Utah, Colorado, and Texas which immediately surround them, as well as by other strong professional schools farther distant. Likewise, Mississippi and Tennessee are surrounded by states having a generous supply of schools offering professional journalism programs; and the New England states without schools of journalism are in comparatively close proximity to Pennsylvania, New Jersey, New York, and Massachusetts, which have a combined group of 13 schools of journalism—five of them members of the AASDJ.

These schools in Group B, although increasing the number of institutions offering instruction in journalism in some of the states, also served by accredited schools, fill in gaps in 13 states which have no AASDJ schools, bringing the total of states containing one or more institutions offering professional training in journalism to 38.

Perhaps the discontinuance of the program of journalism at Grinnell College, in the state of Iowa, in 1941, because of the feeling on the part of the administration that this school would be serving students desiring to enter journalism better by concentration on providing a good liberal background as preparation for their entrance into some strong professional school of journalism, is a trend that will gain momentum in the near future. At any rate, it indicates that serious thought is being given to reorganization in smaller institutions lacking facilities as superior as those found in the larger and better-equipped professional schools, aimed toward the shaping of programs to fit in best with the total educational program of journalism needed. Incidentally, Grinnell was one of the first schools in this group to begin instruction in journalism; its initial program started in 1912.

General enrollment in the institutions containing these Group B schools ranged from a low of 264 at Saint-Mary-of-the-Woods College to a high of 15,447 at the University of California.

TYPES OF ORGANIZATION

Sixty-nine of these schools are in recognized institutions of higher learning; the other two institutions represented are not accredited.

Reports from the schools in this group show that there is a great lack of uniformity in plans for organization within the various institutions. Only 18 are autonomous schools or departments of journalism; 29 are independent departments in the college of liberal arts and sciences; 14 are divisions of English departments; five are in Schools of Business Administration; two are in Schools of Commerce; two are divisions within the School of Science and the Humanities; and one is within the Department of Economics. However, all of them are offering substantial programs in journalism, leading to a degree or a major.

There is no strictly graduate school comparable to the School of Journalism, Columbia University, but one school—Emory University—announced the adoption of the five-year plan in 1941, after the questionnaires used in this study had been returned.

Likewise, requirements for admission vary greatly from institution to institution. A majority of these schools admit students on the freshman or sophomore level, and many of them have set up the same requirements for students of journalism as for all other students seeking enrollment in the college or university as freshmen. Nineteen schools delay entrance until the junior year.

With the exception of those schools admitting students as freshmen, all require satisfactory records in college work done in courses previous to entrance into the program of journalism. West Virginia University requires a "B" average in all freshman and sophomore work. Special requirements in the various schools include the following:

Requirement	No. Schools
Pass Aptitude test	1
Satisfactory completion of introductory courses in journalism	2
Require Freshman English	2
"B" in Freshman English and in introductory courses in journalism	2
Pass comprehensive examination at end of Sophomore year	1
Permission of department head	1
Ability to use typewriter	1
Social Science background required	1

Thus, it may be seen that satisfactory records in college work already done or general admission requirements for entering freshmen serve as the basic determinants for entrance upon professional work in most of these schools.

Insistence upon satisfactory completion of background courses in the social sciences and in other fields before admittance to the professional school —apparent in the requirements of most of the Group A schools—was stressed in only a few of the institutions in this group. This does not mean that courses of this kind are not required for the degree or major, but it does indicate that such work may be taken concurrently with instruction in journalism instead of before admission to the schools is granted.

OBJECTIVES

All 71 schools indicate definite professional objectives, including (1) the preparation of students for positions on newspapers or in allied journalistic fields, and (2) the provision for a wide liberal background for the profession and an understanding of the press as a leading social agency.

Secondary objectives listed included: (1) to provide vocational training for printing, photography, and agricultural and technical writing, given by three schools; and (2) to train high-school journalism teachers, four schools.

REQUIREMENTS FOR GRADUATION

Sixty-seven of the 71 schools in this classification reporting on degree requirements reveal that an average of 22.44 per-cent of the four-year college program must be in journalism courses, leaving 77.56 per-cent of the student's time for liberal background courses.

The average requirement for the bachelor's degree in journalism is 26.5 semester-hours. However, the median for the entire group is 30 hours. The school demanding the highest number of semester-hours in journalism requires 54 hours; the lowest, 16. However, the institution which requires 54 hours offers its journalism courses in a night school whose program closely resembles that of a trade school, and it is not accredited by any official accrediting agency. This is the kind of department which the accredited schools have been discouraging. Although the work in journalism is spread out over more years, the number of hours in professional courses required for graduation in the average school in Group B is approximately the same as in Group A schools. Likewise, the amount of time devoted to background courses outside the schools themselves in other departments is almost parallel.

PROGRAM OF COURSES OFFERED

Based on the same methods for the classification of courses according to content that were described in Chapter III, an analysis of offerings in these schools shows that out of a total of 752 journalism courses given by 64 of the institutions reporting, 66.7 per-cent are on the news side.

A study of individual programs to determine the number of courses offered by each school indicates that the ones with the smallest programs offer only five courses; the one with the largest lists 26.

No. Schools	No. Courses Offered
2	5
3	6
5	7
5	8
9	9
8	10
3	11
7	12
3	13
3	14
3	15
5	16
1	17
3	18
1	19
1	24
1	25
1	26

Complete distribution of all subjects listed—according to content—was found to be as follows:

Type of Course	No.	% of Total
Background	54	7.2
News	501	66.7
Business	116	15.4
Allied	43	5.7
Graphic Arts	38	5.0
Total	752	100.0

Twenty-six of the 66 schools giving information regarding course-offerings include background courses in their programs; all 66 offer most of their work on the news side; 51 have some subjects on the business side; 25 offer courses in allied fields such as radio, short-story writing, publicity, and trade and technical journalism; and 37 give graphic arts courses dealing with typography, photography, or engraving.

With these findings as a basis, course offerings in the average school program in this group would be distributed thus:

Type of Course	No.
Background	.85
News	7.84
Business	1.80
Allied	.67
Graphic Arts	.59
Total	11.75

Reports from 60 schools regarding the total course-hours in journalism being offered show that the average for the group is 36.65 semester-hours, or a median of 35. The number of semester-hours offered by schools in this group ranged from 73 in the school with the highest number to a low of 18 semester-hours.

The school offering 73 semester-hours of work in journalism had five men on the staff. However, three of them were teaching only part time, leaving the equivalent of only three full-time persons to handle the work. Schools giving 18 semester-hours were one-man departments.

A comparison of the program of courses in these schools with those offered by members of the AASDJ reveals some significant facts. In the first place, the Group A schools offer slightly over ten per-cent more background courses, which might indicate that more attention is given to the integration of social sciences and other cultural subjects with journalism work within the schools themselves.

Less stress on the news courses in the Group A schools seems to be shown by the fact that only 48.1 per-cent of their courses are given over to this type of instruction, whereas 66.7 per-cent of Group B schools' program is made up of courses of this type. However, a larger number and variety of courses on the news side are offered in the Group A schools, and their total programs strongly emphasize this phase of training for journalism.

Furthermore, the Group A schools offer a stronger program on the business side, with the average program including 1.9 per-cent more courses of this type than Group B, and 3.8 per-cent more courses in the allied field.

It is apparent that the greatest differences in the average programs offered by the two groups of schools exist in the emphasis placed upon background and business courses.

These schools, like those already accredited by the AASDJ, have attempted to keep pace with new developments within the profession of journalism and in allied fields by adding such courses as photography and radio to their programs. In fact, graphic arts courses, as already pointed out, receive slightly more attention in this group of schools than in the Group A schools.

ENROLLMENT

Fifty-three of the 71 schools furnishing figures for the year 1939–40 showed a total enrollment of 3,695 students, or an average of 70 for each institution represented. As shown in the preceding chapter, Group A schools have an average enrollment of 196.

The plan used in Chapter III of considering all freshmen and sophomores as pre-journalism students and juniors, seniors and graduates as professional resulted in the finding that enrollment was distributed here as follows:

Pre-Journalism	1,984
Professional	1,695
Graduates	16
Total	3,695

Thus, the average professional enrollment in the Group B schools reporting amounted to 32 students as compared with 104 in the Group A schools. Furthermore, the total enrollment in 1939 of these schools was only approximately 58 per-cent as great as that in the 32 schools in Group A. Professional enrollment was approximately half as large.

NUMBER OF GRADUATES

Reports from 51 schools in Group B show that a total of 475 degrees were granted in 1939. This is approximately 35 per-cent as many as were granted by the Group A schools during the same year.

Of this number, 473 were bachelor's and two were master's degrees. No school in this classification offers the doctor's degree in journalism.

Over a three-year period—1937–39 inclusive—these schools turned out a total of 1,293 students, as compared to 3,914 graduated from the Group A accredited institutions. Whereas 333 master's were represented in the degrees given by the latter group, only five were granted by Group B schools.

TABLE 9

NUMBER OF GRADUATES FROM GROUP B SCHOOLS
OVER THREE-YEAR PERIOD

Year	Bachelors	Masters	Total
1937	373	0	373
1938	442	3	445
1939	473	2	475
Total	1,288	5	1,293

Analysis of the figures for the three years shows that there was an increase of 72 students graduated in 1938 over the number receiving degrees in 1937, and that 30 more received degrees in 1939 than in 1938. Over the three years, the increase amounted to 102 graduates, or approximately 26 percent.

The fact that two schools in this group began programs during this three-year period—Kent State University (Ohio), in 1937; and College Misericordia (Pennsylvania), in 1938—accounted for a slight increase. (Kent State University reported graduating seven bachelors in 1938 and five bachelors in 1939; Misericordia did not furnish figures). However, most of the added graduates came from schools already established before 1937.

These findings indicate a trend toward a constantly-increasing number of graduates from the Group B schools, and the addition of two institutions to the group since 1939 might lead to the prediction that output in the future will gradually become larger.

As shown in Chapter III, the number of graduates in the Group A schools increased only 162 over the same period, or 12 per-cent, as compared with the 26 per-cent rise in Group B institutions, which shows that these schools are expanding more rapidly than those in Group A when judged only by the output of graduates over the same period of time.

PLACEMENT OF GRADUATES

Twenty-one of these schools gave no information on the placement of graduates. Reports from 50 institutions on this point show that 322 students receiving degrees in 1939, or 67.7 per-cent of the total number of graduates, found employment.

Of these, 238, or 73.9 per-cent of those placed, went into positions on newspapers; 84, or 26.1 per-cent, were employed in allied journalistic fields such as radio work, publicity, or advertising on publications other than newspapers. (See Appendix E.)

The fact that no figures on placement were given by almost 30 per-cent of the schools might be an indication that none of their 1939 graduates was placed. On the other hand, a school with a very small number of placements may have felt that there were too few to bother about reporting. Some of the schools indicated that no records were kept.

Consequently, it may be assumed that the percentage of placements of 1939 graduates for the entire group of Group B schools would have been slightly higher than 67.7 per-cent if all of them had reported. However, this is only an assumption.

From the figures available, it was found that the number of 1939 graduates from Group A schools receiving employment was 540 greater, and the percentage of placements based upon the total number of graduates was slightly over two per-cent higher in the accredited Group A schools.

The distribution of these placements was practically the same for both groups, with approximately 65 per-cent finding employment on newspapers and 35 per-cent being absorbed in allied journalistic fields.

Although only 41 out of the total 71 Group B schools gave estimates on the distribution of graduates during the past five years, the findings provide a basis for comparisons with Group A.

For instance, approximately the same percentage of graduates from these schools found employment on daily and weekly newspapers. In Group A, 39.75 per-cent went on dailies, as compared with 37.8 per-cent in Group B; and 13.8 per-cent of Group A graduates located on weekly newspapers, against 18.4 per-cent in Group B.

Percentages of absorption were slightly higher in Group B in the magazine, radio, and teaching fields, and lower in press association, syndicate, business publication, and publicity fields. However, in none of these categories was the variation more than 3.4 per-cent. Group A schools indicated a 3.4 per-cent higher absorption in publicity work; in radio work, the Group B schools placed 3.4 per-cent more out of the number reported upon.

The 413 graduates of the 41 Group B institutions over the last five years were found to have been distributed as follows:

Type of Work	No. Placed	% of Total
Daily Newspapers......................	156	37.8
Weekly Newspapers.....................	76	18.4
Press Associations.......................	17	4.1
Syndicates.............................	0	.0
Business Publications....................	12	2.9
Magazines............................	8	1.9
Radio Work...........................	27	6.6
Publicity.............................	39	9.4
Advertising (other than newspaper)........	48	11.6
Other Types (Teaching, etc.)..............	30	7.3
Totals...........................	413	100.0

Since 30 Group B institutions did not give information on this point, the results cannot be regarded as typical of the entire list of 71 schools. However, these findings lead to the conclusion that graduates from both Group A and Group B apparently find employment in similar journalistic fields upon graduation and in about the same proportions.

Again, these facts lead to the conclusion that major emphasis should be placed on preparing students for work on daily and weekly newspapers, with some attention to training for work in allied fields. An investigation of courses offered by these schools, given earlier in this chapter, shows that stress on these aspects of training are being given and that the proportions of emphasis correlate closely with the percentages on placement.

SIZE OF TEACHING STAFF

Sixty-nine schools in this group reported a total of 215 staff members, or an average of three journalism teachers for each institution. However, a breakdown shows that 29 schools have less than three men on the staff, and in 16, only one teacher is engaged in the teaching of journalism. The school reporting the highest number was Emory University, with 11 men on the staff.

Distribution by size of staff and number of institutions is given below:

No. Schools	Size of Staff
16	1
14	2
18	3
9	4
3	5
4	6
2	7
1	8
1	9
1	11
Total 69	215

Many of these staff members have other duties besides teaching journalism. Fifty-one are working newspapermen devoting only part time to teaching; 31 do half or more of their teaching in other fields, including English, history, philosophy, political science, foreign languages, art, music, and commerce. The largest number spend this time teaching English; two have radio duties; 41 devote from one-fourth to three-fourths of their time to publicity; and six spend part time in the University Press offices.

Thus, 131 are teaching only part time in journalism, leaving a total of 84 full-time staff members in the 69 institutions—out of 71—reporting.

After a deduction of the fractions of time being given over to other duties, as indicated by schools furnishing this information, it was found that the average staff in this group consists of an equivalent of 1.9 persons. Breakdowns by institutions on this basis result in these findings:

No. Schools	Size of Staff
6	Less than 1
16	1
12	1 plus
7	2
12	2 plus
9	3
6	3 plus
1	More than 4

A comparison of the size of teaching staffs reveals that the 32 Group A schools employ 43 more members and that the average equivalent full-time staff is larger by 2.8 persons than is that of this group. Furthermore, no school in the American Association of Schools and Departments of Journalism has a staff smaller than 3 men, as compared to 16 one-man staffs in schools in this classification. The Group A school with the largest staff contains two more persons than the school with the highest number of this group.

ACADEMIC RANK OF STAFF MEMBERS

Sixty-nine schools, out of the 71, reporting on the academic rank of staff members indicated that 72, or 33.49 per-cent, are instructors. Professors are next in point of numbers, with 44 reported, or 20.47 per-cent; only 11, or 5.12 per-cent, hold the rank of assistant.

Rank	Number	% of Total
Professor	44	20.47
Associate Professor	20	9.30
Assistant Professor	36	16.74
Instructor	72	33.49
Lecturer	32	14.88
Assistant	11	5.12
Total	215	100.00

As shown by the above table, only 46.24 per-cent of staff members in these schools hold professorial ranks, as compared with 61.63 per-cent in Group A schools. There are 17.6 per-cent more persons with the rank of instructor in this group than in the accredited schools.

Thirty-four of the departments in this group are headed by professors; fourteen by associate professors; twelve by assistant professors; and nine by instructors.

PREPARATION OF STAFF MEMBERS

Methods followed in studying the preparation of staff members in these schools were the same as those used in Chapter III. Academic preparation, teaching experience, and journalistic experience were considered in each instance.

Ninety-two teachers in these schools, or almost 43 per-cent, were found to hold master's degrees; 39 per-cent were bachelors; and 7.91 per-cent held doctor's degrees. Twenty-two persons, or 10.23 per-cent, had no college degrees of any kind.

TABLE 10

ACADEMIC PREPARATION OF STAFF MEMBERS
IN GROUP B SCHOOLS

No. Staff Members	Degrees Held	% of Total
17	Ph.D.	7.91
92	M.A. or M.S.	42.79
84	B.A. or B.S.	39.07
22	No Degree	10.23
Total 215		100.00

The percentage of master's and bachelor's degrees held by staff members in these schools and Group A schools was about the same. However, there were 4.1 per-cent less Ph.D.'s in this group, and the percentage of those having no degrees was over twice as great.

Likewise, staff members appear to have had less teaching experience. Reports from 64 of the 71 institutions resulted in an average of 6.8 years, as compared with 11.3 years of teaching experience in the Group A schools.

Total average journalistic experience was found to be 6.29 years for staff members in the 59 schools giving information on this point. Of this, 5.39 years was newspaper experience and .9 year was in allied fields. However, 17 per-cent of the schools failed to report, and consequently this figure cannot be regarded as accurate for all teachers in the entire group.

The fact that most of the 12 schools not reporting gave all other information, but failed to furnish data on this point, leads to the assumption that most of the staff members represented, if not all, had no journalistic experience. If this were true, the over-all percentage of journalistic experience would be considerably smaller than the foregoing figures indicate.

Furthermore, many years of newspaper experience on the part of a few staff members tended to raise the general average. For instance, three schools had staffs with an average of from 12 to 15 years' newspaper experience, whereas in seven institutions, the teachers had no journalistic experience.

TABLE 11

AVERAGE JOURNALISTIC EXPERIENCE OF STAFFS
IN GROUP B SCHOOLS

No. Schools	Average Years Experience
7	None
11	1– 2
10	3– 4
9	5– 6
6	6– 7
8	8–10
5	10–12
3	12–15

LABORATORY AND LIBRARY FACILITIES

Only 20 of these schools have laboratory facilities that would compare favorably with those provided by AASDJ members. In this respect, only a small percentage could meet the requirements of the AASDJ.

Out of the 57 institutions reporting any kind of laboratories, 34 schools were found to be centering practically all their practice work around the school newspaper or in the university publicity office, where the experience afforded consists of writing and sending out news concerning the institutions.

Only 32 have reporting laboratories and two of these do not provide for editing. The various kinds of laboratories contained in these schools, and their distribution, as listed by schools sending answers, were found to be as follows:

No. Schools	Laboratory Provided
32	Reporting
30	Editing
4	Wire Services
4	Pony or Drop Reports
3	Advertising
9	Typography
9	Photography
3	Radio
1	Engraving
25	Arrangements for reporting laboratory experience with co-operating daily or weekly newspapers.
3	Arrangements for advertising experience with cooperating newspapers.
22	Only school newspaper or publicity office for experience opportunities.

These findings tend to show that in over 45 per-cent of these schools, reporting and editing facilities are not provided. Furthermore, despite the fact that 15.4 per-cent of the average program in these schools is devoted to business courses, only three provide advertising laboratories within the schools themselves.

Under these circumstances, few schools in this group could meet the requirements as set up by the national newspaper organizations and the AASDJ, which called for ample laboratory facilities to carry on the instruction offered in all courses included in the curriculum. This conclusion may be drawn from the fact that although the schools in this group offer a majority of courses on the news side, less than half of them provide reporting and editing laboratories. By contrast, all Group A schools provide completely-equipped city rooms, reporting and news editing laboratories, and in addition several of these also have facilities to take care of other courses offered which require laboratory experience for maximum results.

Library facilities were very much limited in practically all of these schools. Nineteen reported departmental newspaper reading-rooms and limited departmental libraries. Thirty-six have collections of books on journalism in the university or college library, varying from 200 to 850 volumes. Only ten indicate that they get annual appropriations for the purchase of books of journalism for their libraries.

SUMMARY

Although there are 71 schools in this classification as compared to only 32 in Group A, few of them are equipped to offer as thorough and complete a type of training as the latter is providing.

Teaching staffs are smaller and the members' experience—both academic and professional—is inferior to that found in the accredited institutions. This does not mean, however, that none of the staff members in these schools could measure up to those in the other group. Undoubtedly, many persons now employed in these schools have had excellent preparation for the work they are doing, and probably are offering instruction as high in quality as could be found anywhere in the country.

Laboratory and library facilities also are inadequate in most of these schools, which makes it impossible to provide the type of training most in demand by employers, who insist that practical experience should be a part of a student's preparation if he is to be of greatest value to the profession upon graduation.

Although standards for staff and equipment for this group as a whole are not so high as those met by the accredited schools in Group A, as already pointed out, some of these schools are well prepared to give professional training in journalism and are offering sound programs that may be as strong as those found in some of the AASDJ schools.

However, most of the Group B schools are graduating and sending out to be absorbed by the profession men and women who have not had as many of the advantages for a well-rounded and thorough training as can be obtained in the accredited schools holding membership in the AASDJ.

This naturally leads to the assumption that the products of many of these schools are not so well prepared for entering the profession of journalism.

Despite these conditions, the annual increase in percentage of graduates in these schools is much larger than in the Group A institutions, and the rate of increase in the number of schools starting instruction in journalism is considerably higher in Group B. However, the percentage of absorption of graduates by the profession of journalism appears to be only about two per-cent lower in Group B than in Group A schools, which in 1939 produced only 168 less graduates than the total number from both of these groups finding journalistic employment that year.

In addition to the 71 schools in this group and the 32 Group A schools, all of which express definite professional objectives, there are 439 other institutions in this country offering instruction in journalism. Fifty-five of these remaining 439 schools provide substantial courses of study leading to a combined English-Journalism major or to a strong minor in journalism, and on the whole offer a much more limited type of training than the two groups already studied. Classified as Group C institutions, these divisions of journalism will be the basis of the following chapter.

CHAPTER V

GROUP C—OTHER DIVISIONS OF JOURNALISM

UNLIKE the Group A and Group B schools, none of these institutions classified in this study under Group C offers majors or degrees in journalism. Although they are divisions of other departments rather than separate and independent units, a few of the schools in this group are offering broader training for journalistic work than is available in some of the weaker Group B institutions which consider themselves definitely professional in nature.

Institutions in this group include 45 universities and colleges, nine teachers' colleges, and one Negro college.

Figures for the year 1939 from 45 schools showed that three institutions in Group C had a total general enrollment of less than 300; eight, from 300 to 500; 17, from 501 to 1,000; and 17, over 1,000. The University of Pittsburgh had the highest number of students, with 10,500. Notre Dame College (Ind.) and Marylhurst College (Ore.) were lowest—each with a total enrollment of 200.

The purpose of this chapter will be to investigate the work being given by these 55 schools, following as closely as possible the procedures used in preceding chapters dealing with the Group A and Group B institutions. From these findings, an attempt will be made to evaluate the programs in the group in terms of their preparation to carry on professional training for journalism, as compared with the 103 schools already considered.

ORIGINS AND DISTRIBUTION

The State College of Washington was the first Group C school to begin offering instruction in journalism. Initial work was started in 1902, and on June, 21, 1911, special journalism courses upon which the present plan is based were inaugurated.

Before the year 1920, six other institutions in this group had commenced journalism programs. The University of Maine and Bucknell University (Pa.) organized such instruction in 1914; Oregon State College, in 1915; Washburn College (Kans.), in 1917; St. Mary's College, Notre Dame (Ind.), in 1918; and Walla Walla College (Wash.), in 1919. (See Table 12 for the list of all Group C schools and dates on which instruction started.)

Greatest expansion came between the years 1920–30, during which time 22 of the 46 institutions reporting began the work. Seventeen schools started with journalism in the period from 1930–40 (see Graph IV).

Naturally, these figures do not take into account the institutions which may have attempted to establish instruction in journalism but failed, and five of the schools in this group did not report on this point. However, the information received shows definitely what the trend has been.

Since approximately 85 per-cent of the institutions represented did not start work until after the beginning of 1920, at which time several Group A and Group B schools had professional programs under way, they had an opportunity to observe what had been done in the field of education for journalism. Consequently, it is not surprising that most of their present

GRAPH IV

GROWTH OF GROUP C SCHOOLS OF JOURNALISM

(Based on Reports from 46 of These Institutions)

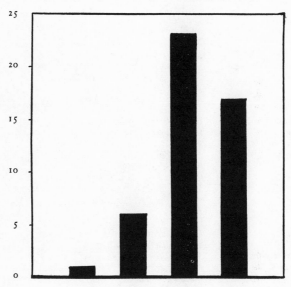

1900–10 1910–20 1920–30 1930–40

programs are modeled closely after those offered in the other two groups considered.

Although the greatest expansion came during the decade 1920–30, more significant is the fact that 15 schools, or more than 27 per-cent, have begun instruction in the last ten years, with one of these starting in 1938 and another as late as 1939.

This indicates that the trend toward a spread of the Group C programs is continuing, but at a slower rate—a condition which would appear to be unwise in the face of the information already presented concerning the Group A and Group B schools, unless these Group C schools were to center their attention on pre-professional objectives.

TABLE 12

GROUP C SCHOOLS WITH DATES OF ORIGIN
OF INSTRUCTION

State	School	Date Instruction Started
Alabama	Alabama Polytechnic Institute	—
Arizona	University of Arizona	—
California	St. Mary's College of Calif.	—
	San Diego State College	1920
Dist. of Columbia	American University	1931
	George Washington University	1937
Florida	University of Miami	1927
Georgia	Wesleyan College	—
Illinois	Mundelein College for Women	1930
	College of Saint Francis	1931
Indiana	Franklin College	1922
	Saint Mary's College, Notre Dame	1918
Iowa	Cornell College	—
Kansas	Kansas St. Teachers College, Pittsburg	1920
	Washburn College	1917
Kentucky	Murray State Teachers College	—
Maine	University of Maine	1914
Massachusetts	Northeastern University	1938
Michigan	Albion College	1920
	Wayne University	1934
Minnesota	College of St. Scholastica	1932
Nebraska	Union College	1929
Montana	Billings Polytechnic Institute	1929
New York	Alfred University	1924
	College of New Rochelle	1925
	Long Island University	1930
	Saint Bonaventure College	1921
North Carolina	Wake Forest College	1923
Ohio	Notre Dame College	1925
	Ohio Wesleyan University	1920
Oklahoma	Phillips University	1928
	Southeastern State College	1924
	Southwestern State College	1923
Oregon	Linfield College	1933
	Marylhurst College	1933
	Oregon State College	1915
Pennsylvania	Bucknell University	1914
	Lincoln University	1939
	Marywood College	1920
	University of Pennsylvania	—
	University of Pittsburgh	1923
	Villa Maria College	—
	Wesminster College	1926
South Carolina	Winthrop College	1936
Texas	Howard Payne College	1924
	North Texas State Teachers Col.	1937

TABLE 12—(continued)
GROUP C SCHOOLS WITH DATES OF ORIGIN
OF INSTRUCTION

State	School	Date Instruction Started
	Southwest Texas St. Teachers Col.	1938
	Texas Wesleyan College	1923
	West Texas State Teachers College	1937
Utah	Utah State Agricultural College	1935
Washington	Eastern Washington College of Educ.	—
	State College of Washington	1902
	Walla Walla College	1919
West Virginia	New River State College	1925*
Wisconsin	St. Norbert College	1933

* Name changed to West Virginia Institute of Technology in 1941.

In the first place, findings on the other two groups show that they are producing more graduates than the profession is able to absorb, and offerings in Group C are not so great nor are the facilities so adequate as found in the other institutions.

Secondly, many of these Group C programs are in states already being served either by Group A or Group B schools—often by institutions in both of these classifications.

In some states, this has happened where there seems to be an over-supply of the better equipped professional schools. For instance, the state of Texas, which contains nine (one Group A school and eight Group B) professional schools, also has five Group C schools, making a total of 14 institutions in all three of these groups offering instruction in journalism.

California, with two Group A and six Group B schools, is found to have two Group C institutions, raising the total to ten; in Pennsylvania, seven Group C schools must be added to the one Group A and five Group B professional schools, for a total of 13 in all; and Iowa is shown to be supporting one Group C school, in addition to two Group A and three Group B institutions—or a total of six.

In Illinois, only two Group C schools have been added to the two Group A accredited institutions, giving this state only four schools represented in these three classifications offering instruction in journalism. None of the four states aforementioned (Texas, California, Pennsylvania, or Iowa) has as many newspapers as Illinois. Texas has 84 less; California, 111; Pennsylvania, 257; and Iowa, 307 fewer newspapers than Illinois. Minnesota, with 502 newspapers, is being served by only one Group A accredited school and one in Group C—a total of two—whereas, Iowa, with only 59 more newspapers, has six schools in these three groups giving instruction in journalism.

On the other hand, Maine, located in a section of the country which contains five states without a Group A or Group B school, does have one institution in the Group C classification offering journalism; and Massachusetts, also in New England has one Group C school as well as one in Group A and another in Group B.

In the deep South, Mississippi is found to be without any school represented in Groups A, B, or C.

Schools in Group C fill in gaps which were apparent in these areas that appeared to need institutions offering some kind of training for journalism, and brings the total of states being served by institutions offering some type of instruction in journalism to 41. Connecticut, Delaware, Mississippi, New Hampshire, Rhode Island, Tennessee, and Vermont have no schools represented in the three groups thus far considered.

However, the District of Columbia, which contains no Group A or Group B institutions, is found to have two Group C schools—located in Washington, D. C. Furthermore, 47 of these Group C programs are being offered in states having accredited Group A schools, which would indicate a tendency for them to originate and to cluster in those areas already being served by strong professional institutions.

It will be shown in this chapter that only a few of the Group C schools —most of them liberal arts institutions—presents a record of placements. Furthermore, they have a tendency to locate in the vicinity of Group A schools. These facts lead to the conclusion that their service to the profession of journalism, in most cases, would be served best by emphasizing pre-professional training aimed toward preparing students for continuing their preparation in the strong professional schools of journalism near them.

TYPES OF ORGANIZATION

As already pointed out, none of these schools offers majors or degrees in journalism. In 41 institutions, the program of journalism is carried as a division of the department of English; in only 14 is the work organized as individual divisions or departments of journalism.

Combined Journalism-English majors or minors in journalism, taken in connection with a major in English, social sciences, business administration and home economics, make up the types of programs offered by most of these schools. In two institutions, the courses in journalism may be counted only as general electives for the bachelor's degree. Two schools failed to give any information on this point.

Six of these schools will not admit students to courses in journalism until the sophomore year; one delays entrance until the junior level; all the rest— approximately 90 per-cent—will admit freshmen who meet the general requirements for admission to the college or university.

The only special requirement, other than those mentioned above, is the stipulation that students be approved by the teacher of journalism, a condition which was mentioned by two of the 55 schools reporting on admission. Background courses in the social sciences and in other fields are taken concurrently with the work in journalism.

OBJECTIVES

Reports from 49 of the schools offering Group C programs show that 42 have definite professional objectives, with the work aimed toward training students for work on newspapers or in allied journalistic fields. Sixteen of these schools indicate that the training of high-school journalism teachers is their secondary objective.

Five institutions list as their major objective the training of teachers for high-school publication work and indicate as their secondary objective the preparation of students to continue with education for journalism in some recognized professional school. However, two of these schools show consistent records of placement of graduates in newspaper work, which tends to indicate that they consider the training given sufficient for graduates who decide to enter the profession upon graduation.

Only two schools in this group indicate strictly pre-professional objectives —the preparation of students to enter other professional schools of journalism where the aim is to train definitely for entering the profession of journalism.

REQUIREMENTS FOR GRADUATION

Reports from 51 of the 55 schools show that 15.4 hours in journalism is the average required in the four-year program. This leaves 84.6 hours, or approximately 87 per-cent of the student's time to be devoted to liberal arts background courses or to other work in related fields elsewhere in the university. This is 11.1 hours less than are required by the average Group B school for a major or degree in journalism.

Thirty-two schools in Group C offer combined Journalism-English majors, with from 12 to 21 hours in journalism and the remainder in English required for the degree. The combination found to be the most common is the requirement of 18 hours of journalism and from 6 to 12 hours of English.

Minors in journalism, offered by 18 Group C schools, range from a requirement of from 8 to 19 hours, with 12 hours being the most general. This may be counted as a related minor, with the major in English, social science, business administration, or home economics.

PROGRAM OF COURSES OFFERED

An analysis of the offerings of 46 of the 55 schools reporting shows that a total of 310 courses were listed. This would make an average of 6.7 courses for each school represented.

The journalism program in 23 of these institutions consists of six or less

courses. The school reporting the smallest number offers only three journalism courses; 13 are being given by the school with the largest program.
Distribution by institution is shown in the following table:

No. Schools	No. Courses Offered
1	3
9	4
4	5
9	6
11	7
2	8
4	9
1	10
3	11
1	12
1	13

As pointed out, the average number of courses offered in Group C is 6.7.
However, exactly 50 per-cent of the schools reporting in this group offer
more courses than this; the other half gives 6 courses or less. Furthermore,
20 of these Group C schools, or slightly over 43 per-cent of those giving information on this point, were found to be offering programs consisting of
from 6 to 7 courses.

Also significant is the fact that 12 of these institutions are giving programs
of journalism as extensive as 55 per-cent of the Group B schools, 35 of
which indicated programs of from 8 to 13 courses.

Twenty-three of the 42 schools reporting offer background courses in
journalism; all 42 give most of their program on the news side; 18 offer one
or more business courses; and 12 give courses in allied fields and the graphic
arts.

Of the 310 courses offered by 46 Group C schools, 237, or 76.5 per-cent,
deal with the writing and handling of news; background courses make up
10.9 per-cent of the program; business courses, 7.1 per-cent; and allied
and graphic arts courses, 5.5 per-cent. The following tabulation shows this
distribution:

Type of Course	No.	% of Total
Background	34	10.9
News	237	76.5
Business	22	7.1
Allied, Graphic Arts	17	5.5
Total	310	100.0

Comparisons with the journalism programs offered by Group B schools
reveals that almost ten per-cent more courses deal with the writing and
handling of news in the Group C schools, and slightly over eight per-cent
more business courses are found in the average Group B program, which

carries only approximately 50 per-cent as many as Group A. Courses in the other three classifications appear in about the same proportion.

These results and the findings on course-offerings in the Group B schools lead to the conclusion that in schools not members of the AASDJ, there is a definite tendency to place more emphasis on news courses and less on those dealing with the business aspects of newspaper publishing.

This undoubtedly is due partly to the fact that staffs are considerably smaller in most of the schools in these two groups and consequently fewer men prepared to handle other types of courses are available to offer the work. Furthermore, with small staffs, it is impossible to offer as many courses and in the case of these schools more news courses appear to have been selected in preference to the other types.

The typical program for Group C, consisting of 6.7 courses, is slightly more than five courses smaller than that typical of Group B. Using the figures already presented as a basis, this typical Group C program would include the five classifications in the following proportions:

Type of Course	No.
Background	.7
News	5.1
Business	.5
Allied, Graphic Arts	.4
Total	6.7

Basing conclusions on the frequency of appearance of courses in the various programs in the Group C schools, it was found that the average program of 6.7 (or 7) courses might be expected to include the following and in the order of preference as listed:

News Reporting
News Editing
Feature Writing
Editorial Writing
Survey course in journalism (such titles as the Contemporary Press, the Modern Newspaper, and Introduction to Journalism were being used for this type of course).
History of Journalism
Advertising

In most schools offering an eighth course, one dealing with The Country Newspaper appeared to be the most popular.

The average school in this group was found to be offering 19 semester-hours of journalism work, as compared with 62 hours in the accredited Group A schools and 36.65 hours in Group B. In other words, the Group A professional school's average program consists of almost 70 per-cent more courses and those in Group B, about 49 per-cent more.

Total hours offered in the 42 schools in Group C reporting ranged from a high of 32 to a low of 7, distributed as follows:

No. Schools	Hours Offered
2	7
7	10–12
15	15–18
11	20–24
7	25–32

ENROLLMENT

Reports from 42 of these schools indicated a total enrollment of 2,301 journalism students in 1939–40, or an average of 54 for each institution represented. As was shown in the preceding chapters, the total average enrollment for Group A schools was found to be 196 and for Group B, 70.

Again, considering freshmen and sophomores as pre-journalism, it was found that there were 1,180 in this classification in Group C; total professional enrollment (juniors, seniors, graduates) amounted to 1,104, and only 17 graduate students were listed by schools giving information on this point. The breakdown is shown below:

Type of Enrollment	No.
Pre-journalism	1,180
Professional	1,104
Graduate	17
Total	2,301

Thus, the total enrollment for 1939 in the Group C programs was only 62.3 per-cent as large as that found in Group B institutions, and the 42 schools in Group C had less than one-third as many students as were en-enrolled in the accredited Group A professional schools.

GRADUATES

Since these schools do not offer a major or a degree in journalism, it was difficult for them to give figures on journalism graduates, and few reported. Only 18 institutions in these groups were able to furnish the information, which was too small a percentage to lead to any trustworthy conclusions.

PLACEMENTS IN 1939

Reports on placements of 1939 graduates were received from only 25 of the 55 Group C schools. Figures from these institutions showed that 80 graduates were placed on newspapers and 45 were absorbed in allied journalistic fields in 1939.

The 13 schools reporting on both the number of graduates and placements were found to have located 66 per-cent of their graduates in some form of journalistic activity.

Again, the information received on this point was too meager for any sound general conclusions other than that a few of the Group C schools are preparing students definitely for the profession and seem to be having fair success in placing graduates upon the completion of the training offered.

However, if the 125 placements reported by schools in this group included all that actually found employment upon graduation from the programs of journalism, the amount of absorption would be insignificant in comparison with the records of placements in Group A and Group B.

The most important finding is that 25 schools in Group C do make an attempt to place their students upon graduation, and 13 of them show a record of placement almost equal to that of the Group B schools.

SIZE OF TEACHING STAFF

Fifty-three schools, out of the 55 in Group C, report a total of 94 staff members. This makes an average of 1.74 persons for each institution, including both those who are teaching full time and those devoting only a part of their time to journalism.

However, since many of these staff-members have other duties besides teaching journalism, the average number of equivalent full-time teachers is less. For instance, out of the 94 staff members reported by the 53 schools, seven are working newspapermen, 33 spend from one-fourth to three-fourths of their time teaching in other fields; 30 spend from one-fourth to seven-eighths of their time on college or university publicity bureaus; and three spend from one-half to three-fourths of their time with the university press.

In all, 73 persons are engaged in other kinds of work in connection with the teaching of journalism, leaving only 21 full-time staff members in the 53 institutions giving information on this point. By deducting the fractions of time allotted to other duties by these 73 persons, the average full-time staff member for these schools is found to be the equivalent of only 1.6 persons.

An analysis of the staffs by this method results in the following findings for the 53 schools furnishing full information:

No. Schools Reporting	Size Equivalent Full time Staff
25	Less than 1
12	1
3	1 plus
7	2
3	2 plus
1	3
2	3 plus

As far as size of full-time staffs are concerned, only three schools out of the 53 measure up to the minimum requirement of the AASDJ, which calls for at least three full-time staff members of professorial rank. In approximately half of the schools in this group, instruction is being given by persons who spend only a portion of their time teaching journalism.

ACADEMIC RANK OF STAFF MEMBERS

Slightly more than 45 per-cent of the staff members in the 53 schools reporting on this point hold the rank of instructor.

The group with the next highest number consists of associate professors, who account for 17.02 per-cent of the total. Professors are third in point of numbers, with 14, or 14.9 per-cent.

Thus, out of a total of 94 staff members in this group, professorial rank is held by only 40, or 42.3 per-cent:

Rank	No.	% of Total
Professor	14	14.90
Associate Professor	16	17.02
Assistant Professor	10	10.64
Instructor	43	45.74
Lecturer	10	10.64
Assistant	1	1.06
Total	94	100.00

Group B schools have 3.94 per-cent more members of professorial rank on their staffs than do Group C institutions, and Group A schools have 19.33 per-cent more.

PREPARATION OF STAFF MEMBERS

The average staff member, as shown by reports from 44 of the 55 schools in this group, has had 8.1 years of teaching experience. Those with the smallest amount had not yet completed their first year of teaching; the person with the highest number had 28 years of teaching experience.

Almost 49 per-cent of the 90 staff members on whom information was given hold master's degrees; 34.44 per-cent have bachelor's degrees; and 13.34 per-cent hold doctor's degrees. Only three persons, or 3.33 per-cent, had no college degree whatsoever. (See table 13.)

TABLE 13

ACADEMIC PREPARATION OF STAFF MEMBERS IN GROUP C SCHOOLS

No. Staff Members	Degree Held	% of Total
12	Ph.D.	13.34
44	M.A. or M.S.	48.89
31	B.A. or B.S.	34.44
3	No Degree	3.33
90		100.00

A comparison of these findings with those on preparation of staff members in Group B schools indicates that the persons in this group have broader academic training. There are 5.43 per-cent more Ph.D.'s in the Group C schools; 6.1 per-cent more master's; and 6.9 per-cent fewer staff members with no degrees. However, there are 4.63 more people holding bachelor's degrees in the Group C schools.

The higher percentage of Ph.D. degrees in these schools perhaps may be accounted for by the fact that many of the staff-members handling courses of journalism also teach college English, a field in which these degrees receive emphasis in the selection of teachers.

Staff-members in 46 schools in this group were found to have had an average of 4.15 years of journalistic experience. Newspaper experience amounted to 3.05 years, and the remaining 1.1 years of experience were in allied journalistic fields.

TABLE 14

AVERAGE JOURNALISTIC EXPERIENCE OF STAFFS
IN GROUP C SCHOOLS

No. Schools Reporting	Av. Years of Experience
13	None
4	Less than 1
6	1– 2
4	2– 3
5	3– 4
6	5– 7
4	8–10
4	10–11
1	17

Here again, it was found that older experienced men in a few of the institutions represented tended to raise materially the general average. Four of these schools' staffs showed an average of from 10 to 11 years. One man alone, of a two-man staff, had over 30 years of newspaper experience to his credit.

However, it will be noted that in 32 out of the 47 institutions reporting, or approximately 70 per-cent, staffs have had less than five years of journalistic experience—the amount required in Group A. Furthermore, in 13 of these schools, or almost 28 per-cent, the work in journalism was being taught by staffs with no journalistic experience whatsoever; and in four schools, or $8\frac{1}{2}$ per-cent, journalistic experience amounted to less than one year. Thus, in a total of 17 Group C institutions, or approximately 36 per-cent of those reporting, the amount of journalistic experience is negligible (see Table 13).

Although the average journalistic experience was found to be 4.15 years for the group as a whole, there appears to be justification for serious doubts on the part of employers in the profession as to the advisability of encouraging many of these schools with their present staffs to attempt to train their students definitely for employment in journalism upon graduation.

LABORATORY AND LIBRARY FACILITIES

Reports from 47 institutions out of the total of 55 in this group indicate that all of them center practically all of their laboratory work around the school newspaper and college publicity office. However, two have advertising laboratories; four have typography laboratories; and four are equipped with photography laboratories.

None of them provides separate laboratory facilities for reporting and editing comparable to those found in many of the Group B and all of the Group A schools, despite the fact that the major part of their course-offerings are on the news side.

In fact, none of these schools appears to have adequate laboratory facilities in any department of the work to carry on the type of professional training desired by leading newspaper organizations and the AASDJ.

Library facilities, as a whole, also are very inferior. Only three schools report having departmental newspaper reading rooms and small departmental journalism libraries. Six indicate that they have fairly adequate journalism sections in their respective college or university libraries.

SUMMARY

None of the 55 schools in the Group C appears to be prepared adequately to offer professional training equal to that prescribed by the leading newspaper organizations and the AASDJ in their Proposed Standards for Schools of Journalism.

In the first place, none of these schools offers majors or degrees, and in only 14 is the work organized as individual divisions or departments. Consequently, even in those institutions in which the stronger programs are offered and where the objectives are definitely professional in nature, the instruction in journalism being given is not in harmony with the accrediting standards.

Furthermore, although course-offerings and their distribution are modeled closely after those of the Group A and Group B schools, the amount of work available is much more limited and none of the schools in Group C has ample laboratory or library facilities to provide the type of training desired by leaders in the profession of journalism.

Full-time teaching staffs in journalism likewise are smaller in most of these schools than would be acceptable by the AASDJ, and although the average academic training is good, it is offset by less than the minimum newspaper experience required in the accredited schools.

In fact, only 15 out of the 47 schools giving information on this point, as already mentioned, had staffs with five or more years of newspaper experience, which means that in a majority of these schools, students are being trained for responsible positions on newspapers by men and women who have had little, or no, practical experience themselves.

Such a situation, in itself, undoubtedly would be frowned upon by employers, who look to schools of journalism to provide them with men and women acquainted with the practical aspects of the business as well as equipped with essential knowledge of the social sciences and other related subjects.

Furthermore, regardless of the fact that the average staff in these Group C schools consists of less than two persons and that many of these teachers are occupied with duties other than journalism, several of them are attempting to provide programs as extensive as those in Group A and Group B, where staffs are considerably larger and better prepared. It seems reasonable to conclude that results under these conditions must be inferior to what can be expected from the Group A and Group B schools.

However, despite their apparent deficiencies, when measured by the existing standards of the AASDJ for professional training in journalism, some of the schools in Group C have shown their ability to place graduates in a profession whose total annual absorption capacity is only slightly larger than could be satisfied by graduates of the recognized professional schools of journalism alone.

Nevertheless, the journalism offerings of the Group C schools in general are considerably broader than those provided by the 384 Group D institutions which will be taken up in the following chapter.

CHAPTER VI

GROUP D—LIMITED PROGRAMS IN
JOURNALISM

SCHOOLS included in Group D are those whose program in journalism
is limited to only a few courses which in most instances are not sufficient to provide a minor in the subject.

Out of a total of 384 institutions in this group, only 37 offer enough work
for a minor; in most of the schools, the courses of journalism are listed
under the English department and may be counted on a major in English.

Represented in Group D are 273 universities and colleges; 91 teachers
colleges; and 20 Negro schools. Reports from 256 of them indicate that 75
per-cent of these schools have general enrollments of 1,000 students or less;
only nine of them have enrollments over 5,000; two have 100.

Schools reporting the smallest general enrollments were Cedarville College (Ohio) and the Tennessee College for Women, with 100 students
each; City College of New York, with a total of 28,000 students, had the
largest enrollment. The complete breakdown was as follows:

No. Schools	Size Enrollment
2	100
42	101–300
62	301–500
85	501–1,000
56	1,001–5,000
9	Over 5,000

Since the programs of journalism carried in most of these schools consist
of only four courses or less, an attempt to compare them with institutions
considered in preceding chapters would be of little value from a qualitative
point of view. Only in cases where evaluation in terms of the former institutions appears to be of special significance will comparisons be made.

The purpose of this chapter will be to investigate these limited journalism
programs and from these findings to draw some conclusions regarding their
apparent ability to accomplish the aims which they express as their major
objectives. Evaluations also will be made in terms of their preparation to
carry on professional training in journalism.

ORIGINS AND DISTRIBUTION

The first school in this group to begin offering work in journalism was
Bessie Tift College (Ga.), which started instruction in the subject as early
as 1898—ten years before the first professional school of journalism was
founded.

However, reports from 281 Group D schools reveal that by the year 1920, only 25—or less than seven per-cent of the present institutions giving information on this point—had commenced the work (see Table 15).

Between 1920-30, a total of 102 Group D schools added journalism programs, but the greatest expansion took place during the period from 1930 to 1940, which saw the rise of 154.

Of significance is the fact that 36 of these schools began instruction in journalism during the three years before this survey was under way— 1938-40, inclusive (see Table 1, Chapter II). This represents almost ten per-cent of the schools reporting, or approximately two per-cent more be-ginnings than had taken place before 1920, and these findings indicate that the introduction of this type of instruction in institutions of higher learning is continuing at a more rapid rate than is being experienced in any of the other three groups of programs. Distribution by periods was as follows:

No. Schools	Date Inst. Started
25	Before 1920
102	1920-30
154	1931-40
Total 281	

The dates on which instruction in journalism started is given in Table 15 for all Group D schools reporting on this point.

These schools are distributed through 44 states and the District of Columbia. (See Appendix F.) Only Delaware, Maine, Nevada, and Wyoming are not being served by institutions offering limited programs in journalism. However, Maine was found to have one Group C school; Nevada, one Group B school; and Wyoming, one Group B institution. Delaware, on the Atlantic coast, near other states containing many schools represented in the four Groups (A, B, C, and D), is the only state in this country which contains no four-year, degree-granting colleges and universities giving instruction in journalism.

Reports on Group D programs in the seven states found to contain no schools considered in Groups A, B, and C, no doubt help to explain why this situation exists. Connecticut is shown to have two Group D programs; Mississippi, seven; New Hampshire, three; Rhode Island, three; Tennessee, fourteen; and Vermont, three. As already pointed out, only Delaware —the other state in this group of seven—is without any type of instruction in journalism. In some of the states where there already appears to be an over-supply of schools offering instruction in journalism additional Group D programs are being offered. For instance, California, shown to have ten schools represented in the other three groups, is found to have 11 of the Group D schools, bringing the total to 21; in Iowa, the addition of 14 Group D institutions, makes a total of 20; Pennsylvania's total is raised to 42 by the inclusion of 29 Group D schools—the greatest number of Group D schools

TABLE 15
GROUP D SCHOOLS AND DATE INSTRUCTION STARTED

State	School	Date Instruction Started
Alabama	Alabama College	1930
	Howard College	—
Arizona	Ariz. State Teachers Col., Flagstaff	1931
	Ariz. State Teachers Col., Tempe	1931
Arkansas	Arkansas A. & M. College	—
	Arkansas College	1938
	Arkansas State College	—
	Arkansas State Teachers College	—
	College of the Ozarks	—
	Henderson State Teachers College	1926
	John Brown University	—
	Ouachita College	—
	Philander Smith College	1937
California	College of the Pacific	—
	Humboldt State College	—
	Mills College	1917
	Mount St. Mary's College	—
	Occidental College	1920
	Pacific Union College	1920
	Pasadena College	1938
	Santa Barbara State College	—
	University of Redlands	1926
	University of San Francisco	—
	Whittier College	1920
Colorado	Adams State Teachers College	—
	Colorado College	1920
	Colorado State College	1919
	State College of Education	1915
	Western State College of Colorado	1924
Connecticut	Albertus Magnus College	—
	University of Connecticut	1918
Dist. of Columbia	Catholic University of America	1932
	Howard University	—
	Miner Teachers College	1932
	Washington Missionary College	1937
	Wilson Teachers College	1931
Florida	Florida A. and M. College	1930
	John B. Stetson University	1935
	Rollins College	—
Georgia	Berry College	1930
	Bessie Tift College	1898
	Brenau College	1928
	Georgia State College for Women	1925
	Oglethorpe University	—
	Shorter College	1934
	South Georgia Teachers College	1932
Idaho	Albion State Normal School	—

TABLE 15—(Continued)

State	School	Date Instruction Started
	College of Idaho	1940
	Lewiston State Normal School	1925
Illinois	Aurora College	—
	Augustana College & Theolog. Seminary	1937
	Bradley Polytechnic Institute	1922
	DePaul University	—
	Eureka College	1940
	Greenville College	—
	Illinois State Normal University	—
	Illinois Wesleyan University	—
	Lake Forest College	1938
	Loyola University	1928
	MacMurray College for Women	1924
	McKendree College	—
	Monmouth College	1925
	North Central College	1930
	Northern Illinois State Teach. College	1924
	Rockford College	1933
	Rosary College	1925
	Shurtleff College	1930
	Southern Illinois Normal University	1936
	The Principia College	1934
	Wheaton College	1931
	Western Illinois State Teach. College	1923
Indiana	Ball State Teachers College	1925
	Central Normal College	1932
	DePauw University	1937
	Earlham College	1929
	Evansville College	1919
	Hanover College	—
	Huntington College	—
	Indiana Central College	—
	Indiana State Teachers College	1936
	Purdue University	1915
	Valparaiso University	1928
Iowa	Buena Vista College	1930
	Clarke College	—
	Iowa State Teachers College	1929
	Iowa Wesleyan College	1919
	Loras College	1939
	Luther College	1927
	Morningside College	1910
	Parsons College	1939
	St. Ambrose College	1934
	Simpson College	1919
	Upper Iowa University	—
	Wartburg College	1938
	Western Union College	1928
	William Penn College	1930

TABLE 15—(Continued)

State	School	Date Instruction Started
Kansas	College of Emporia	1924
	Fort Hays Kansas State College	1922
	Kansas State Teachers College, Emporia	1912
	Kansas Wesleyan University	1923
	Marymount College	1927
	Mount St. Scholastica College	1930
	Ottawa University	1920
	Southwestern College	1922
	St. Mary College	—
Kentucky	Asbury College	—
	Bowling Green College of Commerce	—
	Eastern Kentucky State Teachers College	—
	Georgetown College	1938
	Kentucky Wesleyan College	1938
	Nazareth College	1925
	Transylvania College	1935
	Union College	—
	University of Louisville	1933
	Western Kentucky State Teachers College	—
Louisiana	Centenary College	1929
	Louisiana College	1930
	Louisiana State Normal College	1920
	Southern Univ. and A. & M. College	1920
	Southwestern Louisiana Institute	1936
	Ursuline College	—
Maryland	Blue Ridge College	—
	Hood College	1922
	Maryland College for Women	—
	Washington College	—
	Western Maryland College	1930
	St. Joseph's College	1915
Massachusetts	American International College	1934
	Atlantic Union College	—
	Calvin Coolidge College	1937
	Eastern Nazarene College	1936
	Emerson College	1925
	Mount Holyoke College	1918
	Regis College	1934
	Simmons College	1927
	Springfield College	1935
	State Teachers College	1928
	Tufts College	1924
	Wellesley College	1920
	Wheaton College	1935
Michigan	Adrian College	1920
	Alma College	1930
	Central State Teachers College	1930
	Cleary College	1938
	Detroit Institute of Technology	1935
	Emmanuel Missionary College	1919

TABLE 15—(Continued)

State	School	Date Instruction Started
	Ferris Institute	1933
	Kalamazoo College	1929
	Northern State Teachers College	1937
	Siena Heights College	—
	Michigan State Normal College	—
Minnesota	Augsburg College & Seminary	—
	Carleton College	1920
	College of St. Catherine	1935
	College of St. Thomas	1920
	Concordia College	1936
	Gustavus Adolphus College	1929
	Hamline University	1918
	MacAlester College	1930
	St. John's University	1938
	St. Olaf College	1923
	State Teachers College, Bemidgi	1930
	State Teachers College, Duluth	1939
	State Teachers College, Moorhead	1928
	State Teachers College, St. Cloud	1932
	State Teachers College, Winona	1931
Mississippi	Alcorn A. & M. College	—
	Delta State Teachers College	—
	Mississippi College	—
	Mississippi Southern College	1937
	Mississippi State College	1932
	Mississippi State College for Women	—
	University of Mississippi	1939
Missouri	Central Mo. State Teachers College	1915
	Culver-Stockton College	—
	Lincoln University	—
	Lindenwood College	1923
	Missouri Valley College	—
	Southeast Mo. State Teachers Col.	1933
	St. Louis University	1928
	Teachers College of Kansas City	—
	William Jewel College	—
Montana	Carroll College	1937
Nebraska	Doane College	1922
	Duchesne College	—
	Nebraska Central College	—
	Neb. State Teachers College, Chadron	1921
	Neb. State Teachers College, Kearney	1925
	Neb. State Teachers College, Wayne	1921
	Nebraska Wesleyan University	—
	Peru State Teachers College	1924
	University of Omaha	1928
	York College	1927
New Hampshire	Dartmouth College	1929
	Keene Teachers College	1938
	Rivier College	—

TABLE 15—(Continued)

State	School	Date Instruction Started
New Jersey	College of Saint Elizabeth	1918
	Georgian Court College	—
	New Jersey State Teachers Col., Jersey City	1940
	New Jersey State Teachers Col., Montclair	1932
	New Jersey State Teachers Col., Newark	1937
	Seton Hall College	—
New Mexico	New Mex. State College	—
	New Mex. State Teachers College	1939
	University of New Mexico	1929
New York	Brooklyn College	1938
	Colgate University	1932
	College of Mount St. Vincent	—
	City College of New York	1936
	Good Counsel College	1930
	Hartwick College	1930
	Houghton College	1936
	Hunter College of the City of New York	1934
	Nazareth College	—
	Niagara Uinversity	1929
	Notre Dame College of Staten Island	1938
	Russell Sage College	1933
	Sarah Lawrence College	1928
	St. John's University	1938
	St. Joseph's College for Women	—
	St. Lawrence University	—
	University of Buffalo (Millard Fillmore College)	1923
	University of Rochester	1929
	Wagner Memorial Lutheran College	1933
North Carolina	Elon College	1926
	Flora MacDonald College	—
	Greensboro College	1928
	Lenori Rhyne College	1940
	Queens College	1924
	Woman's Col. of the Univ. of No. Car.	1920
North Dakota	North Dakota Agric. College	1921
	State Normal and Industrial School	1936
	State Teachers College, Dickinson	1930
	State Teachers College, Mayville	1938
	State Teachers College, Minot	1922
	State Teachers College, Valley City	—
Ohio	Alfred Holbrook College	1934
	Antioch College	—
	Ashland College	—
	Baldwin-Wallace College	1937

TABLE 15—(Continued)

State	School	Date Instruction Started
	Cedarville College	—
	College of Mount St. Joseph	—
	Denison University	1919
	De Sales College	1936
	Fenn College	1934
	Miami University	1910
	Muskingum College	—
	Ohio Northern University	1925
	Otterbein College	1930
	University of Akron	1921
	University of Cincinnati (Evening)	1926
	University of Dayton	—
	University of Toledo	1921
	Ursuline College	—
	Western College	1921
	Western Reserve Univ. (Adelbert Col.)	—
	Wilberforce University	—
	Wittenberg College	1923
	Xavier University Downtown College	—
	Youngstown College	1935
Oklahoma	Agricultural and Normal University	1936
	Catholic College of Oklahoma	1933
	Central State Teachers College	1920
	East Central State College	1940
	Northeastern State College	1923
	Northwestern State College	1929
	Oklahoma College for Women	1924
	Panhandle Agric. & Mech. College	1924
	University of Tulsa	1923
Oregon	Pacific College	1937
	Pacific University	1936
	Reed College	1939
	University of Portland	—
	Willamette University	1922
Pennsylvania	Albright College	—
	Allegheny College	1925
	Beaver College	1935
	Cedar Crest College	1932
	Chestnut Hill College	1931
	Dickinson College	1935
	Drexel Institute of Technology	—
	Duquesne University	1926
	LaSalle College	—
	Moravian College	1934
	Moravian College for Women	1936
	Muhlenberg College	1915
	Pennsylvania College for Women	1935
	Rosemont College	—

TABLE 15—(Continued)

State	School	Date Instruction Started
	Seton Hill College	1918
	State Teachers College, Bloomsburg	1939
	State Teachers College, California	1932
	State Teachers College, Clarion	1939
	State Teachers College, East Stroudsburg	1937
	State Teachers College, Edinboro	1939
	State Teachers College, Indiana	1935
	State Teachers College, Kutztown	—
	State Teachers College, Lock Haven	1937
	State Teachers College, Shippensburg	—
	State Teachers College, Slippery Rock	1939
	State Teachers College, West Chester	—
	Susquehana University	1931
	Ursinus College	—
	Washington and Jefferson College	1919
Rhode Island	Providence College	1938
	Rhode Island College of Education	1930
	Rhode Island State College	1934
South Carolina	Allen University	1938
	Claflin University	—
	Clemson College	1925
	Furman University	—
	Lander College	1934
	Newberry College	1938
	State A. & M. College	1913
South Dakota	Augustana College	1925
	Dakota Wesleyan University	1916
	Northern State Teachers College	—
	Sioux Falls College	—
	Yanktown College	1930
Tennessee	Cumberland University	—
	King College	—
	Knoxville College	1929
	LeMoyne College	1939
	Lincoln Memorial University	—
	Madison College	1933
	Southwestern	1939
	State Teachers College	1930
	Tennessee Agric. & Ind. State College	1920
	Tennessee College for Women	1923
	Tennessee Polytechnic Institute	—
	Union University	—
	University of Chattanooga	1925
	University of Tennessee	1928
Texas	Abilene Christian College	—
	Agric. & Mech. College of Texas	1938
	East Texas State Teachers College	—
	Houston College for Negroes	1935

TABLE 15—(Continued)

State	School	Date Instruction Started
	Incarnate Word College	1935
	McMurray College	1926
	Prairie View State College	1930
	Sam Houston State Teachers College	1937
	St. Edward's University	—
	St. Mary's University	1927
	Southwestern University	1925
	Sul Ross State Teachers College	1930
	Texas College of Arts & Industries	1927
	University of Houston	1930
	University of San Antonio	—
	Wiley College	1935
Utah	University of Utah	1930
Vermont	St. Michael's College	1937
	Trinity College	—
	University of Vermont	1916
Virginia	Lynchburg College	1934
	Madison College	1924
	Mary Baldwin College	1932
	Mary Washington College	1924
	Roanoke College	1939
	State Teachers College, East Radford	1927
Washington	College of Puget Sound	1925
	Gonzaga University	—
	Seattle Pacific College	1930
	Western Washington Col. of Education	—
	Whitman College	1919
	Whitworth College	1925
West Virginia	Bluefield State Teachers College	1928
	Concord State Teachers College	1935
	Davis and Elkins College	—
	Fairmont State Teachers College	1929
	Glenville State Teachers College	1929
	Morris Harvey College	1936
	Salem College	—
	Shepherd State Teachers College	1921
	West Liberty State Teachers College	1930
	West Virginia State College	1930
	West Virginia Wesleyan College	1933
Wisconsin	Beloit College	1932
	Carroll College	1933
	Milton College	1926
	State Teachers College, LaCrosse	1920
	State Teachers College, Milwaukee	—
	State Teachers College, Platteville	1938
	State Teachers College, River Falls	1930
	State Teachers College, Superior	1933
	State Teachers College, Whitewater	1928

GRAPH V

GROWTH OF GROUP D SCHOOLS OF JOURNALISM

(Based on Reports from 281 of These Institutions)

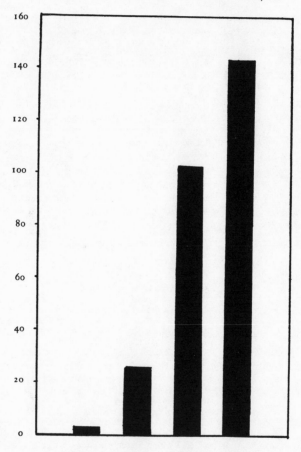

Before 1910   1910–20   1920–30   1930–40

found to be in any one state in this country; and Texas, with 16 Group D schools, also has 13 others—only one of which is a member of the AASDJ —for 30 in all.

Two states—Utah and Montana—have only one Group D school each. However, Utah also has one Group B and one Group C institution, and in Montana there is one Group A and one Group C school in addition to the Group D school.

The tendency of the Group D schools also to cluster in the largest numbers within states containing strong Group A professional schools is apparent. All of these states contain one Group D school or more, and thirteen of them—California, Illinois, Iowa, Indiana, Massachusetts, Michigan, Minnesota, New York, Ohio, Pennsylvania, Tennessee, Texas, and West Virginia—have more than ten Group D programs in addition to the Groups A, B, and C schools represented in each.

This condition may have arisen because of the encouragement lent these Group D institutions by the apparent success which schools in the other groups were experiencing in the field of education for journalism. Still another possible cause may have been the feeling, on the part of most of the Group D institutions, of a need for programs that would prepare students for entrance into strictly professional schools of journalism after the first two years, or upon graduation.

This would appear to be the most logical function of programs in Group D, since most of them are located in liberal arts institutions, where curricula aimed toward providing a broad cultural background for journalism could be organized. In fact, findings which will emerge farther along in this chapter tend to indicate that this very thing is being done by many of the Group D institutions.

TYPES OF ORGANIZATIONS

In only six of the 384 institutions in this group is the instruction organized in independent departments of journalism. Three carry courses of journalism as a division of commerce or business; in two, the work is given in the department of education; and in one, it is offered by the division of agriculture. The remaining 372 schools offer journalism as courses in English departments.

Two of these schools permit courses in journalism to be counted on majors in education; four give credit for journalism on majors in business administration; and 362 allow courses in journalism to be counted on the English major. In the other six institutions, journalism may serve only as general electives.

As already pointed out, only 37 offer enough work to constitute a minor, and none of them offers majors or degrees in journalism. Consequently, the level of admission to journalism courses—from the standpoint of professional training—has little meaning, since the question of determining the matter rests in departments other than journalism in all except six schools.

OBJECTIVES

Professional objectives similar to those expressed by Group A and Group B schools and departments of journalism are indicated by only 30 out of 313 schools in Group D reporting on this point. Below is a summary of objectives, as expressed by these schools:

Objective	*No. of Schools*
1. Definitely professional, aimed toward preparing students for entrance into journalistic work upon graduation..........................	30
2. Pre-professional, with courses in journalism providing definite motivation for English...	137
3. Training of teachers for secondary school publication and supervision and for providing them with an understanding of the press as a leading social agency...	78
4. Training of college newspaper staffs and for providing motivation for writing..	68
Total reporting...	313

It will be noted in addition to the 30 schools with professional objectives, in 137 of the Group D schools, the journalism program is considered as pre-professional, with the work directed toward the motivation of work in English courses. Only 79 of these schools, indicating professional or pre-professional objectives, show any consistent record of placement of graduates in journalistic fields, despite efforts apparently being made to train definitely for entrance into the profession.

The training of teachers for secondary-school publication supervision and the need of providing them with an understanding of the press as a leading social agency are listed by 78 institutions as their primary objective.

Sixty-eight schools offer courses in journalism for the single purpose of training college-newspaper staffs and of motivating the student's writing for these publications. Some expressed the opinion that the ability to write, thus gained, would be of benefit to graduates who might decide to enter the profession, but they offered this as a secondary consideration.

PROGRAM OF COURSES OFFERED

Out of a total of 319 schools reporting on this point, it was found that 177, or over 55 per-cent, offer only one course in journalism. Four courses or less are given by 309 of the institutions.

The largest number offered by any institution was 7 courses, given by only one school in the group. Tabulation of these findings is as follows:

No. Schools	*No. Courses Offered*
177	1
71	2
34	3
27	4
5	5
4	6
1	7
319	

On the basis of returns obtained, it was found that a total of 585 courses are being offered in 319 schools, or an average of 1.5 courses for each.

Judging from a study of course descriptions provided, this average program consists, first of all, of a course in news writing.

In practically every school, news writing is the first one listed. This is particularly true where the program consists of only one course. If the program consists of two courses, the second one most frequently found is feature writing. Next in order of preference as the second course in a two-course program is copy editing; however, often it will be a course combining a study of advanced news writing (with practice provided), copy reading and editorial writing. Few schools give any business courses such as advertising, or those in allied fields, especially if the program is limited to three or less courses.

Although some schools in this classification with a program of only one or two courses include one dealing with "background" material, this type of offering is noticeably lacking. When such a course does occur in the curriculum, it usually is one dealing with a history of American journalism or a survey course, incorporating information on history, ethics of newspaper publishing, certain social aspects, and instruction on the construction of the news story, supplemented by practice in writing.

The most common practice apparent in practically all of the programs of journalism in this group is that of attempting to crowd a number of subjects into a two- or three-hour course, generally labelled as "news writing." A typical description of such a course reads as follows:

NEWS WRITING—In this course the student will take up a study of the American newspaper and its history; news-writing and reporting (practice in writing news articles, the editorial, feature articles and reviews); editing of the news; and a consideration of typographical makeup of the modern newspaper.

In the Group A accredited professional schools and in those in Group B, each of the subjects listed here under the one heading of "News Writing" generally is taken up in a separate course, with at least as much time devoted to each as is given over for a study of all the subjects in the single course typical in Group D schools.

Background courses dealing with the social aspects of newspaper publishing, ethics, contemporary affairs, public opinion and the like—which one might expect to find in small programs in liberal arts colleges—are offered in only a small number of the Group D schools. This condition leads to the assumption that here many of these schools are overlooking perhaps their greatest opportunity to serve the profession of journalism. Although lacking the necessary curriculum, equipment and staff to carry on sound professional training, most of these institutions are in a position to give a wide cultural background.

As already mentioned earlier in this chapter in the discussion on objectives, 137 out of the 313 reporting on this point apparently are attempting to provide pre-professional programs, stressing this type of training, and another 146 stated that this is one of the major aims. Thus, a total of 283 of these institutions now recognize this opportunity to be of greatest service in the training of journalists.

However, an investigation of their course-offerings reveals that there is considerable confusion as to what the nature of a pre-professional program should be and a great lack of uniformity in courses offered. In many of the schools, considerable emphasis is placed on professional courses in journalism that are available in professional schools far better equipped for such work. This is especially true in the case of technical courses requiring laboratory and library facilities. On the other hand, most of these schools are well prepared to provide thorough training in grammar and composition and a good grounding in the social sciences and in courses dealing with the rôle of the press in society—the type of education considered essential in pre-professional programs aimed toward preparing students for entrance into recognized professional schools of journalism. Furthermore, this type of program would be highly desirable for students not planning to enter the profession of journalism, especially if it were supplemented by courses directed toward teaching students how to read newspapers and how to interpret news.

ENROLLMENT

Reports from 189 schools furnishing figures on enrollment in journalism courses resulted in the following findings:

Freshmen and Sophomores	2,141
Juniors and Seniors	2,868
Graduates	28
Total	5,037

This is equivalent to an average enrollment of 26 students for each of the institutions reporting. Twelve of these students would be freshmen or sophomores and 14 would be juniors or seniors.

There was a wide variation in the number of students indicated by the various institutions, with the figures ranging from a low of only three at Roanoke College and Mary Washington College, in Virginia, to a high of 200 students at Whitewater (Wisconsin) State Teachers College. Altogether, seven out of the 189 schools giving this information reported enrollments of over 100.

GRADUATES AND PLACEMENTS

Reports on graduates were too scattered to have any meaning for the group as a whole. Furthermore, since none of the schools in this classification offers majors or degrees, there are no graduates strictly in journalism. Most of the students take their major in English, including from one to four courses in journalism.

Only seventy-nine schools—all of them from the group indicating definite professional or pre-professional objectives—gave information on the placement of 1939 graduates. It was found that, altogether, 134 of their graduates found employment. Eighty-one of these went on newspapers; 53 were absorbed in allied journalistic fields.

The fact that 305 schools in this group failed to report any placements does not mean necessarily that none of their graduates found employment within the profession of journalism. However, it is probable that the percentage of their graduates absorbed by the journalism profession is very low.

In the case of the 79 schools giving placement figures, it was revealed that the average number of graduates finding employment in 1939 was 1.7 for each institution.

SIZE AND PREPARATION OF STAFF

A total of 319 staff members was reported by 306 of the 384 schools in this group. However, most of these teachers of journalism devote much of their time to teaching in other fields—such as English—and to work in the publicity department of the college or university where they are employed.

It was found that the average teacher in this group devotes less than half of his time to the teaching of journalism, and the average full-time staff for the 319 institutions, after deductions for other activities are made, amounts to .4 person. In other words, each school has an average of one teacher devoting .4 of his time to journalism and .6 to other duties.

From the 298 schools giving information regarding the journalistic experience of teachers, it was found that the average for these staffs was 2.2 years. However, this average for the group as a whole was made possible only by the fact that in a few of the institutions there were some seasoned newspapermen with from 15 to 30 years of journalistic experience—a situation which aided materially in raising the general average.

The findings on journalistic experience of staff-members in Group D is given in the following summary:

No. Schools	Av. Yrs. Jour. Experience
166	None
19	Less than 1
44	1– 2
19	2– 4
17	4– 6
11	6– 8
15	10–15
7	20–32
298	

For the most part, the Group D staffs had very little, if any, practical newspaper experience. A total of 166, or almost 56 per-cent of the 298 schools reporting, indicated that their teachers had no journalistic experience whatsoever, and in 19 institutions, or over 6 per-cent, the staffs had less than one year. Altogether, approximately 62 per-cent of these teachers had less than one year or no experience at all.

Furthermore, if reports had been available from the 86 schools in this group that failed to give information, it is probable that this percentage would have been even higher.

Only about ten per-cent of the schools giving information reported staffs with experience equivalent to the minimum required by the Group A professional schools.

However, despite this situation, the Group D schools are attempting to teach journalism, and 79 institutions in the group show definite records of placement of students who are trained mainly by one person possessing inadequate practical experience, who spends over half of his time in activities other than the teaching of journalism.

LABORATORY AND LIBRARY FACILITIES

Only 26 of the 384 schools indicate that they have laboratory facilities—and these are very meager. Most of the laboratory work centers around publishing the campus newspaper or working in the college or university publicity office.

The fact that 358 gave no information on this point might be taken to indicate that in these schools the instruction in journalism is given only by the lecture method, supplemented perhaps by assignments on much the same plan as that followed in teaching courses in English.

Library facilities for journalism likewise appear to be missing in all except 24 of the schools in this group. Only this number reported having libraries, which ranged from a few texts and reference-books to small collections of books on journalism in the college or university libraries. The largest such collection reported consisted of 300 volumes. One school indicated that its entire library facilities consisted of a dictionary, and a directory which was shared with the English department.

From these findings, it may be seen that library and laboratory facilities in the Group D schools reporting are very inadequate. In fact, the reports would indicate that text books owned by the students themselves make up the "library" in most instances.

SUMMARY

In no sense can the schools in this group be considered adequately prepared to offer professional training as defined by the AASDJ in its Standards for Schools of Journalism. In the first place, they lack the type of organization required, and offerings are far too limited.

Most of them also could not meet the requirements on necessary newspaper experience of staff-members. The average staff-member, based on reports from 298 schools, was shown to have only 2.2 years newspaper experience, but even more significant is the fact that in over half of the schools giving information on this point, instruction in journalism is being given by men who have had no journalistic experience whatsoever.

Even in these institutions where the staffs have had considerable newspaper experience and the necessary academic training, laboratory and library facilities are not available for the purpose of putting theory into practice—a requisite regarded as highly essential by leading newspapers.

Since schools in Group D are not equipped with both professionally trained staffs and adequate laboratory and library facilities, it seems obvious that they should not attempt to offer professional courses in journalism aimed toward preparing students for entrance into the profession. Furthermore, professional schools of journalism generally refuse to recognize the transfer of credits in courses of journalism taught by teachers unqualified by practical experience and training in journalism to handle such subjects.

Even in the institutions in this group which aim to prepare teachers for work in secondary schools as supervisors of publications, the adequacy of a program which includes a maximum of four or five courses in journalism typical of those in Group D is to be questioned seriously. Far better preparation for this kind of work undoubtedly could, and should, be obtained in recognized professional schools.

Located as most of them are in colleges of liberal arts, these Group D schools no doubt could serve the profession of journalism best by reshaping their programs to provide non-professional courses in journalism and other related background subjects for the purpose of preparing students for entrance into the recognized professional schools.

A program of this type might include courses dealing with the press as a social institution, the history of journalism, journalistic writing, and the interpretation and evaluation of newspapers and news. In addition, a wide selection of courses in the social sciences and related subjects should be required.

Such preparation thus afforded would be desirable for students who do not expect to follow journalism as a career, as well as for those planning to enter the profession after the completion of sound training in the well-equipped professional schools of journalism.

At the same time, they perhaps would be making their greatest contribution toward raising the standards of the profession of journalism in this country by concentrating effectively on one of the most important phases in the development of professional journalists.

CHAPTER VII

SUMMARY OF FINDINGS

SCHOOLS OFFERING JOURNALISM

THIS STUDY of the four groups of colleges and universities in the United States offering instruction in journalism has resulted in some significant findings regarding the number of institutions engaged in training men and women for journalistic careers.

Blanketing the country from the Atlantic to the Pacific are 542 institutions of higher learning giving programs of journalism of various types. They are distributed throughout 47 states and the District of Columbia.

This situation bears out the prediction by members of the National Council on Professional Education for Journalism before this study was undertaken that a high percentage of colleges and universities in this country were engaged in education for journalism.

A breakdown of the number of schools serving these five professions resulted in the following findings:

Profession	Total Schools	No. Accredited
Law	180	104
Medicine	No figures	77
Engineering	155	118
Dentistry	No figures	39
Journalism	542	32

Thus, the assumption that professional schools of journalism outnumber institutions serving the professions of law, medicine, engineering, and dentistry appears to be well-founded.

By comparison, in 1939 there were 180 law schools in the United States, 104 of which were on the approved list of the American Bar Association; and 118 undergraduate curricula in engineering, out of a total of 155 engineering schools inspected, were on the accredited list.

At the same time, the medical profession was being served by 77 schools accredited by the American Medical Association. Only 39 dental schools were on the American Dental Association's approved list.

While the number of accredited schools of journalism is lower than in the other professional fields mentioned, this situation does not appear to have held down the total number of institutions offering instruction in journalism, as seems to have been the case in the other fields. This leads to the conclusion that there is a need for pre-journalism programs comparable to the pre-medical and pre-law programs.

For instance, if all of the pre-law programs were added to the 180 law schools now serving that profession, the total number undoubtedly would be very large. Yet, the aim of the pre-law program clearly is not to train students for entrance into the profession of law upon completion of the work offered in schools giving this preliminary instruction. Rather, its purpose is to give students a type of education that will prepare them for entrance into the recognized professional law schools.

On the other hand, many of the 542 schools offering small programs in journalism consider themselves capable of preparing students definitely for professional work and are placing in positions graduates who have not had the advantage of sound professional training available in the accredited institutions which are adequately prepared to carry on this type of program.

These schools equipped to offer the smaller, more limited programs undoubtedly could perform a far greater service in the field of education for journalism by providing pre-journalism training aimed toward giving students a rich cultural background and perhaps an introductory course in journalism in much the same manner as pre-law or pre-medicine programs provide essential courses which form the basis for carrying on work in these professional schools.

Each of these professions has been struggling with the problem of raising educational standards for many years and still has many obstacles to overcome. The Council of the American Medical Association was organized in 1904, the American Bar Association Standards of Legal Education were adopted in 1921, the Engineers' Council for Professional Development was organized in 1932, and the Council on Dental Education began its activities in 1909.

In each instance, the schools and leading organizations of the professions represented have cooperated closely in efforts to improve conditions.

Similarly, the National Council on Professional Education for Journalism was organized for like purposes, but its formation did not come about until 1939, although the Joint Committee began activities aimed toward the formation of a national group in 1930. The fact that nation-wide efforts did not get under way until many years later than any of the other four professions mentioned no doubt accounts partially for the apparent lack of progress in the matter of accreditment and the raising of standards among schools of journalism.

What has been accomplished in the case of law, medicine, engineering and dentistry should help to serve as a guide for the National Council on Professional Education for Journalism in its decisions on future steps to be taken for the improvement of education for journalism in the United States.

The major consideration of these professions in their efforts to improve instruction has been that of limiting the number of professional programs to those schools able to meet standards regarded as essential for sound training.

If the number of accredited schools in these professions can be regarded as criteria worthy of serious consideration by journalism, it seems probable that one of the major, and immediate, goals of the National Council representing the profession of journalism and the schools serving it should be

MAP I

GEOGRAPHICAL DISTRIBUTION OF THE 542 FOUR-YEAR, DEGREE-GRANTING COLLEGES AND UNIVERSITIES IN THE UNITED STATES OFFERING INSTRUCTION IN JOURNALISM

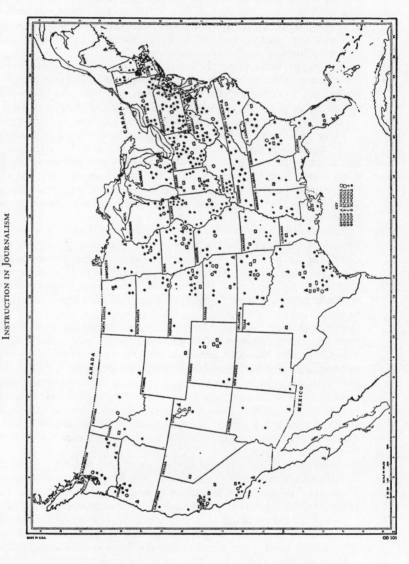

that of encouraging a decrease—if not a limitation by the enforcement of standards of accreditment—in the number of schools offering professional training in journalism.

Dr. F. L. Mott, dean of the School of Journalism, the University of Missouri, and a member of the National Council on Professional Education for Journalism, has this to say regarding the problem:

What are the controls over inferior education for journalism? The Council on Education of the AASDJ can exert some control upon the Class A schools and some upon those of Class B. But the area of acute danger is that which is represented by the 42 Class C and 30 Class D schools which claim to have "professional objectives." They are attempting terminal education for journalism without being staffed or equipped for such work. They are the chief sinners in the whole program. Is there any control which will be effective against them?

Law and medicine have the licensing leverage; but licensing, the historic enemy of liberty of the press, can never be used in connection with preparation for journalism. Protests directed to college administrations can be expected to have only a limited effectiveness. The best control is, obviously, the education of employing newspapermen with regard to the difference between inadequate, flashy, and sham training on the one hand, and approved curricular, staff, and laboratories on the other. This education of employers is not easy, since old prejudices, local preferences, and matters of individual personality always figure large in employment; but it is necessary to undertake it, and this is, I believe, logically the next step in the program of the National Council on Professional Education for Journalism.[1]

The 32 accredited schools in Group A, in 1939, produced 1,352 graduates, or an average of 42 for each institution. Total absorption of graduates of schools of journalism by the 184 schools giving information on this point was found to be 1,439 for 1939.

In other words, the 32 Group A accredited schools appear to have produced almost as many graduates in 1939 as the profession of journalism absorbed from all of the schools included in this study which gave information on placements. Furthermore, one more school—Emory University—has been accredited by the AASDJ since that time. This will bring this group of professional schools still closer to adequately meeting the demands of the profession. Consequently, no great increase in the number of accredited professional journalism schools appears to be warranted at the present time. As the need arises, new members of the American Association of Schools and Departments of Journalism undoubtedly should be drawn from the stronger Group B schools able to meet the requirements for admission.

This does not mean that the remaining Group B, Group C, and Group D schools offering journalism instruction should be discontinued. On the other hand, they would have a highly important function to perform in providing college students an understanding of the press as a social instrument and in

[1] Personal letter from Dr. F. L. Mott, dean of the School of Journalism, University of Missouri, Columbia, Mo., March 22, 1944.

furnishing vital background material essential in the preparation of students for entrance into strong professional schools equipped to offer the highest type of journalistic training.

ORIGINS AND GROWTH

Beginning with a plan for the introduction of instruction in Washington University (now Washington and Lee University) in Virginia, in 1869, education for journalism has experienced a rapid, mushroom-like growth during the intervening years. In slightly more than seven decades, every state in this nation, with the exception of Delaware, has seen the rise of instruction in journalism in one or more institutions of higher learning.

The greatest expansion came in the last decade—from 1930 to 1940. One hundred seventy-six schools—or over 42 per-cent of the 415 institutions reporting dates of origin—began programs in journalism during this period. Of particular significance is the fact that all of the 32 Group A schools and 62 out of 71 in Group B had been established before 1930. In other words, more than 91 per-cent of these institutions, all of which express definite professional objectives, have been engaged in education for journalism for more than ten years. In fact, the last Group A professional school to establish the work began its program in 1929; 30 of them had programs under way before 1920.

TABLE 16

DISTRIBUTION OF DATES OF ORIGIN OF INSTRUCTION
FOR 415 SCHOOLS REPORTING

Group	1869–1908	1909–19	1920–29	1930–40	No. Reporting
A	13	17	2	0	32
B	0	10	37	9	56
C	1	6	22	17	46
D	1	25	105	150	281
Total	15	58	166	176	415

Over half of the Group B programs began between 1920–29, during which period 37 started instruction in journalism. None of these had been established by 1908—the year in which the first professional school of journalism in this country opened at the University of Missouri. However, three years later, in 1912, the first institutions in this group started the work and by the end of 1919, instruction in journalism was being offered by 10 Group B schools.

These facts seem to indicate that the successful development of Group A schools played some part in influencing the other institutions considered in Group B to organize programs in journalism. Likewise, these same considerations, together with the growing interest demonstrated by Group B schools, undoubtedly influenced the rise of instruction in journalism in Group C institutions, since only one program in this classification was under way before 1909. Six were established from 1909–19; 22, from 1920–29; and the remaining 17 came during the period 1930–40. Although the development here was slower, a peak was reached during the 1920's, and the trend continued until 1939, during which year the most recent of these Group C programs was started.

On the other hand, Group D schools, offering limited programs, experienced their greatest growth during 1930–40, when instruction in journalism was begun in 150 institutions, or over 53 per-cent of the schools in this group reporting on dates of origin.

Particularly significant is the finding that 74 of the 415 schools in all four groups which gave information on this point began programs of journalism during the last five years—1936–40 inclusive—and that five of these, all Group D institutions, started in 1940.

Distribution of beginnings during this five-year period (1936–40 inclusive) was found to be as follows:

Group A	0
Group B	3
Group C	7
Group D	64
Total	74

This shows that the trend toward the establishment of instruction in journalism in colleges and universities is continuing at a rapid rate. Furthermore, by far the greatest development is taking place in institutions that are not adequately prepared to carry on the type of professional training advocated by the National Council on Education for Journalism—a situation which emphasizes strongly the necessity for discouraging further expansion.

If order is to be maintained, prompt attention should be given to effective methods of accreditment aimed toward the stiffening of standards and the readjustment of programs in many institutions if the greatest utilization of all instruction now being offered by the 542 institutions engaged in education for journalism in this country is to be realized.

GEOGRAPHICAL DISTRIBUTION

The largest number of colleges and universities offering instruction in journalism in the United States is located in the Eastern half of the country, with greatest concentration occurring in the Middle East and Mid-West. Only one state—Delaware—has no school offering instruction in journalism; 25 states and the District of Columbia have 10 or less; 14 have from 11–19; and seven have 20 or more.

There is a gradual thinning out in the Western area and in certain sections in the South. However, California, on the West coast, has a total of 21 schools, and Texas, in the deep South, is being served by 30 colleges and universities giving instruction in journalism.

This grouping of many schools in some states also is evident in the Mid-West and in the East. For instance, Illinois has 26; Iowa, 20; and Ohio, 30. In New York, there are 26; and in Pennsylvania, 42—the largest number found in any one state in the nation.

However, only two institutions in Illinois are Group A schools; there are none in Group B. Twenty-two are limited programs in institutions represented in Group D. Thus, out of this state's total of 26, just two are schools indicating definite professional objectives, and both of these are members of the American Association of Schools and Departments of Journalism. They are Northwestern University and the University of Illinois.

In California, Iowa, Ohio, Pennsylvania, and Texas the situation is somewhat different. California has eight schools represented in Groups A and B; Iowa has five; Ohio, four; Pennsylvania, six; and Texas, nine. New York, with a population more than twice as large as any of these states, with the exception of Pennsylvania, is being served by only three strictly professional journalism schools, all of them Group A accredited institutions.

The distribution of the four types of programs in these seven states which contain more than 20 institutions offering instruction in journalism is shown in the following table, together with figures on population and the number of daily and weekly newspapers for each:

State	Number of Programs				Total Number	Population	No. Daily and Weekly Newspapers
	A	B	C	D			
California	2	6	2	11	21	6,873,688	757
Illinois	2	—	2	22	26	7,874,155	868
Iowa	2	3	1	14	20	2,535,430	561
New York	3	—	4	19	26	13,479,142	808
Ohio	1	3	2	24	30	6,907,612	530
Pennsylvania	1	5	7	29	42	9,900,180	611
Texas	1	8	5	16	30	6,414,824	784
Total	12	25	23	135	195	53,985,031	4,919

These seven states alone contain $37\frac{1}{2}$ per-cent of the Group A schools, approximately 39 per-cent of Group A and Group B schools combined, and almost 36 per-cent of the 542 schools offering instruction in journalism in the United States.

If these institutions were distributed on a population basis, this allotment perhaps would be about right, since the seven states under consideration have a combined population equivalent to 41 per-cent of that of the entire continental United States, which amounted to 131,669,274, according to the 1940 census.

Likewise, the distribution, if based on percentages of newspapers located in this group of states, would be equitable, since they support 38 per-cent of the nation's 12,875 daily and weekly newspapers being published in 1940.

However, further analysis reveals that New York and Illinois, with a combined total of 1,676 daily and weekly newspapers, or 34 per-cent of the total represented in all seven states in this grouping, together have only five Group A and Group B professional schools. Add to this the fact that states near New York, including Maine, with only one institution—a Group D school—offering instruction in journalism, and Delaware, which has no school of journalism of any kind, and it is apparent that these two states (New York and Illinois) seem to be meeting the needs and demands of their particular areas with fewer professional schools of journalism than any other combination of two states represented, despite the fact that their combined total of dailies and weeklies is far greater than any other pair of states in this grouping.

For instance, Pennsylvania, with only 36 per-cent as many newspapers as New York and Illinois, has one more school represented in Groups A and B and only ten less schools classified in all four groups (A, B, C, and D).

With just 45 per-cent as many newspapers, California has eight professional schools classified in Groups A and B, as compared with the five in Illinois and New York. Texas has nine Group A and Group B institutions— or over 64 per-cent more—yet this state contains 84 less newspapers.

Iowa, with five professional Group A and Group B schools—the same number as found in New York and Illinois together—has only approximately 37½ per-cent as many newspapers, but it should be noted that whereas all of the five schools in the latter states are Group A institutions, three of the five in Iowa are Group B.

Likewise, although Ohio has one less Group A school than Illinois, this state's total of four Group A and Group B institutions is double the number of schools in these two classifications found in Illinois; yet Ohio has 238 less newspapers than Illinois.

These facts seem to indicate that at least five of these seven states, when judged from the standpoint of size and number of newspapers served as compared with the number of professional schools, already are over-supplied with institutions offering professional training for journalism, and the additional Group C and Group D institutions in all of these states add to the problem.

There is a strong tendency for institutions represented in Groups B, C, and D to cluster around the accredited Group A schools. A breakdown reveals the following situation:

State	No. Group A Schools	No. All Others (Groups B, C, D)
California	2	19
Colorado	1	8
Georgia	1	10
Illinois	2	24
Indiana	1	16
Iowa	2	18
Kansas	2	13
Kentucky	1	11
Louisiana	1	9
Massachusetts	1	15
Michigan	1	16
Minnesota	1	16
Missouri	1	9
Montana	1	2
Nebraska	1	14
New Jersey	1	7
New York	3	23
Ohio	1	29
Oregon	1	8
Oklahoma	1	15
Pennsylvania	1	41
Texas	1	29
Virginia	1	6
Washington	1	9
Wisconsin	2	11
Total	32	378

In every state containing a Group A school, other institutions also offering instruction in journalism are to be found, with the number ranging from a low of three such schools in Montana to a high of 41 in Pennsylvania.

The extent of this concentration is emphasized by the finding that in these 25 states containing Group A schools, 378 other institutions out of the total of 542 in this country, or almost 70 per-cent are engaged in education for journalism. Add to these the 32 Group A schools, and it is found that over 75 per-cent of the nation's 542 schools offering instruction in journalism are located in these 25 states, leaving 23 others with no accredited journalism schools and a much smaller percentage of B, C, and D programs.

This naturally leads to the conclusion that some sections of the country today are being served more adequately than others by strong schools of journalism.

On the other hand, in the more thinly-populated areas where this condition exists, states without Group A schools apparently are being cared for by accredited professional schools in adjoining states. For instance, although Idaho, Wyoming, Utah, and New Mexico contain no Group A schools, they are adjoined by other states with accredited schools.

Nevada and Arizona, with only one Group B institution, one in Group C, and two in Group D, are near California, which has two accredited Group A institutions and 19 others classified in Groups B, C, and D.

Oregon, with one Group A institution, three Group C, and five Group D—a total of nine schools—borders Nevada on the north. Although New Mexico has only three schools, all in Group B, it adjoins Texas, which has one Group A school and 29 others, and also touches the Panhandle of Oklahoma, a state with one Group A institution and 15 others included in Groups B, C, and D.

In the North, North Dakota and South Dakota have no Group A institutions, but together they have three group B institutions and 11 Group D programs; furthermore, they are surrounded by Iowa, Minnesota, Nebraska, and Montana, each of which contains one accredited Group A school or more.

The southern section of the country, embracing Arkansas, Mississippi, Tennessee, Alabama, Florida, North Carolina, South Carolina, Louisiana, and Georgia, is being served by only two Group A accredited schools, one of which is located in Louisiana and the other in Georgia.[2] However, some of the other states represented in this area contain Group B institutions that offer strong programs. Arkansas has two Group B schools; Albama, one; Florida, four; Louisiana, three; Georgia, two; South Carolina, one; and North Carolina, one.

Another section, in New England, consisting of the states of Maine, Vermont, New Hampshire, Connecticut, and Rhode Island has no Group A or Group B professional schools. However, these states are near New York, Massachusetts, Pennsylvania, and New Jersey, all of which contain strong Group A accredited professional schools. Consequently, there appears to be no immediate need for the development of more professional schools in this area.

The most urgent need at present appears to be that of encouraging a decrease in the Group B, Group C, and Group D institutions which today are attempting to carry on professional programs of journalism that fail to measure up to the standards approved by the National Council on Profes sional Education for Journalism—or a readjustment of these programs. In this direction seems to lie the major answer to the problem of improvement in the quality of instruction in journalism offered in the colleges and universities of the country.

PRESENT TYPES OF ORGANIZATIONS

Of the 465 institutions reporting on the types of organizations now in operation, it was found that 175 express definite professional objectives; 51 more show consistent records of placement.

[2] Since Emory University (Ga.) was admitted to membership in the American Association of Schools and Departments of Journalism in December, 1941, this section now has three accredited professional schools.

However, in only 99 of these 226 schools is the program of journalism organized as an independent school or department. All the rest are divisions of other departments or consist of one course or more in other departments in the colleges and universities represented. The distribution of these schools and departments is as follows:

	Sch. or Dept.	Total Schools
Group A	32	32
Group B	47	71
Group C	14	55
Group D	6	384
	99	542

Only approximately 18 per-cent of the 542 institutions offering instruction in journalism in this country are organized as schools or departments. Furthermore, the 32 Group A and the 71 Group B schools are the only ones giving degrees or majors in journalism. The remaining 439 institutions' offerings consist of majors combining journalism and some other subject (usually English), minors, or of one course or more which might count as general electives for the bachelor's degree.

The 99 schools whose programs are organized as separate academic units are all that could meet the requirements proposed in the Standards for Journalism adopted by the National Council. As already pointed out, only 103 schools (those in Groups A and B) out of the total of 542 offer degrees or majors in journalism.

LEVEL OF ADMISSION

Twenty-five Group A schools admit students at the junior level; one (Northwestern) delays entrance until the senior year; and one (Columbia), organized as a graduate school, will accept only those students who already have earned the bachelor's degree. Thus, 27 out of the 32 schools in this group require two years of preparation before granting admittance to the professional school.

By contrast, only 19 of the Group B schools delay entrance until the junior year; the majority of these institutions admit on the freshman or sophomore level; many of them setting up the same requirements for journalism students as those which apply to liberal arts.

Approximately 90 per-cent of the Group C schools admit freshmen. Only seven indicate that they delay entrance until the sophomore year, and one accepts students on the junior level.

In all except six of the 384 Group D schools, the courses in journalism are carried in other departments, where admission to courses is controlled.

Thus, only 47 schools, out of the total of 542 offering journalism instruction, require two years of college work before admittance, a condition which the National Council recommended in its new standards for professional training. Of these, 27 already are members of the AASDJ.

REQUIREMENTS FOR GRADUATION

From 120 to 140 hours of credit are required for graduation in most of the 542 institutions studied. In Group A and Group B schools, an average of approximately 23 per-cent of this amount, or about 28 credit-hours of the work leading to the bachelor's degree must be in journalism, leaving 77 per-cent of the student's time for devotion to background courses in the liberal arts and sciences. Approximately 16 hours, or 13 per-cent of the total, must be in journalism in the average Group C schools.

Since the average Group D school offers an equivalent of only 1.5 courses in journalism, which serve in practically every instance as electives, no definite general requirements for these schools can be determined, and, if possible, would have little meaning.

Although the Proposed Standards for Schools of Journalism do not specify the number of credits in journalism that should be required for the degree or major, the fact that the present members of the AASDJ require an average of 29.1 hours indicates that approximately this number would be regarded as satisfactory.

On this basis, only the Group A and Group B schools could qualify. The average school in Group C requires 16 hours, or approximately half this amount, and Group D schools fall far below the requirements set up in Group C.

PROGRAMS OF COURSES OFFERED

Findings on course offerings reveal that the Group A schools' average program consists of 23.4 courses; Group B, 11.75 courses; Group C, 6.7; and Group D, 1.5.

The Group A school with the smallest program offers only 12 courses—a number about the same as the average for Group B. Furthermore, 29 of these Group B schools offer 12 or more courses. The institution with the largest program offers 26.

Apparently, 29 of the Group B schools might meet the requirements of the AASDJ on the size of program offered.

In Group C, one school offers 12 courses, and one offers 13; all the rest give less than the minimum found in the AASDJ.

Since the average in Group A is 23.4 courses, those schools now holding membership in the AASDJ with less than this amount probably should be encouraged to increase the size of their programs. However, the quantity of courses alone should not serve as the basis of accreditment; naturally, what the courses contain is of first importance from an educational point of view, so long as sufficient variety is provided to assure a rounded program of training for journalism.

Distribution of courses according to content in all four groups was found to be as shown in Table 17 below.

Of particular significance is the fact that a much higher percentage of background courses is offered in Group A schools than in any of the others.

In this connection, it should be pointed out that these Group A institutions require only 23 per-cent of credits to be earned in journalism out of the total of 120–140 required for graduation, which allowed strong emphasis to be placed on the provision for a broad liberal education as preparation for students planning careers in journalism.

Compared to the 17.6 per-cent of background courses found in the average Group A program, that of Group B contains only 7.2 per-cent, and the average program in Group C has 6.7 per-cent less than that in Group A

TABLE 17

TYPES OF COURSES OFFERED IN THE 319
SCHOOLS REPORTING

Type of Courses	Group A	Group B	Group C	Group D
Background	17.6%	7.2%	10.9%	.08%
News	48.1	66.7	76.5	99.90
Business	17.3	15.4	7.1	.01
Allied	9.5	5.7	5.5	.01
Graphic Arts	7.5	5.0	—	—
No. Schools Reporting	32	64	46	319

schools. The number of background courses offered in Group D is too small to have any significance.

The percentage of news courses is 18.6 per-cent greater in Group B than in Group A. The average Group C program contains 28.4 per-cent more, and over 99 per-cent of the courses of journalism in Group D schools deal with news.

Both Group A and Group B schools devote over 15 per-cent of their work to business courses; but the Group C schools offer less than half as many business courses as either Group A or Group B, and the schools in Group D give practically no attention to this phase of training, despite the fact that findings on placements indicate that a high percentage (41 per-cent in the case of Group A) of graduates find employment requiring a knowledge of the business end of newspaper publishing.

The average program in both Group A and Group B schools contains over ten per-cent of Allied and Graphic Arts courses, whereas Group C schools offer less than half as many of this type of course, and attention to these phases in Group D again is insignificant.

Basing observations on findings concerning the types of offerings made in all four groups, it appears probable that Group B schools, all of which offer degrees or majors in journalism, should devote a much higher proportion of their attention to background courses, and those schools in Group C with professional objectives which are desirous of offering the type of training desired most by the profession should increase offerings of this type.

By neglecting courses in the Graphic Arts, the Group C schools are over-looking another phase of training which the leading journalistic organizations consider essential.

As already pointed out, it would seem that Group D schools could best serve the profession by centering their attention on providing programs that would give students a wide background of liberal training designed to prepare them for entrance into strong professional schools. On the contrary, at the present time, information on course offerings from 319 schools in this group indicates that very few background subjects are being offered in the average program, but that practically all of their work is on the news side. This situation exists, despite the fact that they lack adequate laboratory and library facilities and that the average staff consists of the equivalent of only .4 person, who has had less than half of the five years of newspaper training recommended by the National Council. In fact, a large number of staff members in the Group D schools have had no journalistic experience whatsoever.

Readjustment of the average program in Group D schools, with a view toward shaping one that would best serve the interests of the profession, would result in one heavily weighted with background courses and carrying a small percentage of news courses aimed primarily toward motivating the student's work in English composition and at the same time toward developing his ability to write clearly and concisely. Probably only those schools equipped with adequate laboratories should attempt to go much farther than this, since they are faced by handicaps that make it impossible for them to provide the kind, or quality, of training in the news end that can be obtained in recognized professional schools. Furthermore, schools in Group D, as well as some in all of the other classifications, should be encouraged to build up journalism libraries.

These conclusions on the types of programs desirable for schools offering instruction in journalism appear to be in complete agreement with those of the National Council on Professional Education for Journalism which were stated in its initial report on findings obtained in the national survey as follows:

The National Council on Professional Education for Journalism recognizes the value of giving college students an understanding of the press as a social instrument and as an agency vital in the functioning of our democracy; it recognizes that journalistic techniques may be effectively employed in motivating an interest in English composition and creative writing courses; that Teachers Colleges may find a course in Supervision of School Publications a necessary part of the training of prospective secondary school teachers. It recognizes furthermore that a broad liberal arts education is the best foundation for professional education for journalism.

It therefore believes that many of the institutions now offering courses in journalism may play a part in the program of education for journalism by developing pre-journalism programs with a strong emphasis on English and the social sciences, incorporating some objective study of the press and perhaps some introduction to journalism through special English courses, and social studies.

In the light of the facts disclosed by this survey, however, the National Council believes that there are more institutions attempting to provide professional education for journalism than placement opportunities in all journalistic fields warrant.

It believes that no institution should attempt to offer a program of professional education for journalism unless it can provide an adequate staff with the necessary educational qualifications and a minimum of five years of practical journalistic experience and unless it can also provide adequate laboratory, library, and teaching facilities.

AVERAGE STAFFS

In connection with any proposed program of journalism for Group D schools, it must be borne in mind that few men in these institutions have had enough journalistic experience to qualify them for teaching technical courses, when using as a basis the standards set up by the National Council which call for an average of at least five years.

Reports on this point from 298 Group D institutions revealed that the average staff-member had only 2.2 years of journalistic experience, and furthermore, that this average staff consists of an equivalent of only .4 person.

However, these staff-members appear to have had sufficient academic training and teaching experience to assure unusual success in providing background liberal arts courses, regarded so highly essential today in the training of men and women for entrance into the profession.

Size of the average full-time staff in each of the four groups studied was as follows:

Group A	4.7 persons
Group B	1.9 persons
Group C	1.6 persons
Group D	.4 person

All except two schools in Group A have staffs with an average of five or more years of journalistic experience. These two have only slightly less than five years.

In Group B, 31 schools, out of the total of 71, reported staffs with an average of five years or more, although the average for the entire group answering is 6.29 years of journalistic experience.

Only 15 of the schools in Group C have staffs with an average of five or more years of journalistic experience, and the average for the group as a whole is 4.15.

The average Group D staff, as already pointed out, has an average of 2.2 years of journalistic experience.

These figures, of course, do not reveal the fact that some men in all four groups have had many years of experience, a condition which raised the group averages in every instance. However, the results do show where deficiencies seem to exist.

Staffs in each of the four groups, with few exceptions, have sufficient academic preparation and teaching experience. However, only 78 institutions out of the total of 542 investigated could meet the requirements on size of staff recommended by the National Council. Thirty-two of these schools already are members of the AASDJ, 31 are in Group B, and 15 are Group C schools.[3] Furthermore, in addition to the 32 accredited schools, just 16 schools in Group B, and three in Group C have equivalent full-time staffs of three or more persons, the number recommended as a minimum for schools offering professional training for journalism.

A lack of sufficient laboratory and library facilities in some of these institutions, and other deficiencies already pointed out, would prevent them from being able to meet the requirements of the AASDJ.

Only ten institutions not now members of the national organization appear to be almost able to fulfill the standards proposed by the National Council. All the others would have to strengthen their programs in certain aspects in order to qualify.

This leads to the conclusion that one of the next steps in the attempt to raise standards of professional training in journalism should be that of investigating intensively the institutions most nearly meeting the requirements, with a view toward recommendations which, if followed, would lead eventually to the admittance of a few more schools into the American Association of Schools and Departments of Journalism if the need for such additions arises.

Steps in this direction naturally should be taken cautiously, with strong efforts at the same time to encourage those schools without adequate staffs and equipment to readjust their programs along lines that would result in the provision of basic background training aimed toward the preparation of students for entrance into the recognized professional schools.

In this way, editors and publishers might come to look with greater confidence to the professional schools in our colleges and universities for recruits of the highest type, and the number of poorly equipped "journalism" graduates would be diminished greatly.

ENROLLMENT, GRADUATES, PLACEMENTS

A growing need for immediate steps toward raising standards in education for journalism is emphasized by findings on the number of graduates and their absorption by the journalistic profession.

Reports from 316 of the 542 schools reveal that in the year 1939, a total of 17,395 men and women were enrolled in journalism; 9,031 of these students were juniors, seniors, and graduates. If the number attending those institutions which failed to give information on this point were added to this figure, the total probably would be around 22,000.

Findings on graduates obtained from the 32 Group A schools and 51 Group B institutions showed that in 1939, these 83 produced 1,827 gradu-

[3] These figures are based on reports received before Emory University (Ga.) was admitted to the AASDJ in December, 1941.

ates. Figures from the remaining 459 institutions, if they were available, no doubt would raise this total materially.

However, none of the Group C and Group D schools offers majors or degrees in journalism, and consequently their graduates could not be regarded strictly as graduates in journalism. Nevertheless, as already pointed out, reports on placement indicate that many of these institutions place graduates in the field of journalism.

Placements in the year 1939 amounted to 1,439 in the 184 schools reporting. They were distributed as follows:

Group A	862
Group B	318
Group C	125
Group D	134
Total	1,439

Approximately 40 per-cent of these graduates came from schools not members of the AASDJ; over 15 per-cent were graduates of Group D institutions, where staffs and equipment are very inadequate for professional training.

This total of 1,439 represents the equivalent of approximately one journalism graduate for every nine daily and weekly newspapers being published in this country in 1940, which seems extremely low. However, the fact remains that the number of students graduated by the Group A and Group B institutions in 1939 exceeded the number absorbed by the journalistic profession from all four groups by almost 400.

Only approximately 60 per-cent of these came from the Group A accredited institutions whose programs are known to meet the requirements of the National Council. A total of 259, or 18 per-cent, was graduated from schools in Group C and Group D which do not offer degrees or majors in journalism and whose facilities, for the most part, are not adequate for carrying on the type of training for journalism recommended by the National Council on Professional Education for Journalism in the Proposed Standards for Journalism Education.

RECOMMENDATIONS FOR IMPROVEMENT

The foregoing summary of information presented in this study answers the questions raised which seemed significant in discovering the types of programs being given in those four-year, degree-granting colleges and universities in the United States which offer instruction in journalism and in evaluating the various programs in terms of their provisions to carry on professional training in journalism, according to the standards set up by the American Association of Schools and Departments of Journalism.

The stress placed on the need for standards of accreditment as a means of improving instruction in journalism has been made always with the end-product—the journalism graduate—in mind. For, after all, changes in curricula, in methods of instruction, in laboratory and library facilities, and in staffs of instruction, unless aimed toward the ultimate goal of producing a higher type of graduate and thus assuring resultant improvement in the quality of the American press as a great social institution, would be useless from an educational standpoint.

Findings made on the development of education for journalism from its beginning and on its present status in colleges and universities in this country today offering this work show the gradual improvement in the quality of offerings that has been made and demonstrate that the preparation of students for work in the field of journalism has been greatly strengthened generally. However, further changes and readjustments appear to be necessary if the greatest utilization of present programs for the betterment of education for journalism is to be accomplished. Constant changes in our complex society naturally call for corresponding changes in the type of education best suited for those who are to have a major part in the perpetuation and in the improvement of the service of the American press to its people.

Results of this investigation indicate that the interests of education for journalism in the United States might be served best if these recommendations were followed:

1. In order to avoid an undesirable surplus of journalism graduates and to insure adequate training for those receiving degrees, in addition to the accredited Group A schools, only the institutions in Group B providing the more adequate programs should be encouraged to carry on professional training with a view to eventually seeking admission to the American Association of Schools and Departments of Journalism, since those professional schools now accredited appear to be capable of furnishing almost enough graduates annually to satisfy the demands of the profession for trained workers.

2. The schools in Group B providing the less adequate programs and all of the institutions in Group C and Group D now offering instruction in journalism should be strongly encouraged to readjust their programs to provide pre-journalism training aimed to afford a rich cultural background in the social sciences and some introductory courses in journalism as preparation for entrance into the accredited journalism schools.

3. All of the schools now offering instruction in journalism should be encouraged to cooperate closely in building up a coordinated program of education for journalism in the United States which would result in graduates of the highest caliber—men and women able to live up to the growing demands and to the best traditions of their calling.

4. The next step in the efforts of the National Council on Professional Education for Journalism to raise standards should be the sponsorship of an intensive, thorough-going, qualitative study of the accredited Group A schools and of the Group B schools most nearly meeting the requirements for admission to the American Association of Schools and Departments of Journalism. Such an investigation should consist of a minute examination of the curriculum, classroom methods, staff members and their qualifications to teach, and other important considerations bearing on the instruction in journalism being offered in each of these institutions to supplement and expand the data already brought together in this study.

This would involve the appointment of a committee made up of representatives from the leading newspaper organizations and of outstanding educators in journalism whose purpose would be that of visiting each school to observe and to examine the work being done, followed by critical evaluation.

Out of such an undertaking might come a new classification of schools investigated and recommendations for final accreditment of only those institutions found to be offering the soundest programs. As a result, the weaker Group A schools could be given specific suggestions on how, and where, to strengthen their programs in order to retain their present rating. It might mean that some of the schools now members of the AASDJ would be replaced by institutions in Group B found to be offering stronger programs.

Furthermore, there should emerge a clarification of standards essential to the greatest improvement of education for journalism and a much needed plan for regular systematic inspection and appraisal of the work being offered by the accredited professional schools of journalism, as well as by those desiring admission to the AASDJ when additions might be warranted—a plan similar to that followed by other leading professions in this country.

In this way, editors and publishers might come to look with confidence to the professional schools for graduates capable of serving with distinction as workers in the American press, and the confusion now existing might be replaced by a more orderly program of professional education for journalism in this country.

BIBLIOGRAPHY

BOOKS

BLEYER, WILLARD GROSVENOR. *Main Currents in the History of American Journalism.* New York: Houghton-Mifflin Co., 1924.

EATON, THEODORE H. *Education and Vocations.* New York: John Wiley & Sons, Inc.; London: Chapman & Hall, Limited, 1926.

MACNEIL, NEIL. *Without Fear or Favor.* New York: Harcourt, Brace & Co., 1940.

WILL, ALLEN SINCLAIR. *Education for Newspaper Life.* Newark, N. J., The Essex Press, 1931.

WILLIAMS, SARA LOCKWOOD. *Twenty Years of Education for Journalism.* Columbia, Mo.: E. W. Stephens Publishing Co., 1929.

WINGATE, CHARLES F. *Views and Interviews on Journalism.* New York: F. B. Patterson, No. 32 Cedar Street, 1875.

YOST, CASPAR S. *The Principles of Journalism.* New York: D. Appleton & Co., 1924.

PERIODICALS AND PUBLICATIONS[1]

ALLEN, E. W. "Journalism as Applied Science," *Journalism Quarterly*, IV (1927), 1.

CASEY, RALPH D. "Journalism, Technical Training and the Social Sciences," *Journalism Quarterly*, IX (1932), 31.

Catalog, Graduate School of Journalism, Columbia University (1939–40), 8.

Catalog, Medill School of Journalism, Northwestern University (1939–40), 14.

"Directory of Teachers of Journalism in Colleges and Universities in the United States," *Journalism Quarterly*, IX (1932), 104.

"Directory of Teachers of Journalism in Colleges and Universities in the United States," *Journalism Quarterly*, XI (1934), 110.

"Directory of Teachers of Journalism in Colleges and Universities in the United States," *Journalism Quarterly*, XIII (1936), 226.

"Editorial," *The Journalism Bulletin*, IV (1927), 25.

HARRINGTON, H. F. "Teaching of Journalism in a Natural Setting: An Application of the Project Method," *Educational Administration and Supervision*, Vol. 4 (1919), 198.

HYDE, GRANT M. "The Next Steps in Schools of Journalism," *Journalism Quarterly*, XIV (1937), 35.

"Journalistic Education in the United States, 1926–27," *The Journalism Bulletin*, IV (1927), 9.

"Journalistic Education in the United States, 1928–29," *Journalism Quarterly*, VI (1929), 1.

LEE, JAMES MELVIN. *Instruction in Journalism in Institutions of Higher Education.* U. S. Bulletin No. 21, Department of Interior, Bureau of Education, 1918.

LUXON, NORVAL NEIL. "Trends in Curricula in A.A.S.D.J. Schools," *Journalism Quarterly*, XIV (1937), 353.

MURPHY, LAWRENCE W. "Professional and Non-Professional Teaching of Journalism," *Journalism Quarterly*, IX (1932), 46.

[1] Complete list of college and university catalogs used for collection of data has been omitted.

NASH, VERNON. *Educating for Journalism*, Published Doctoral Dissertation, Teachers College, Columbia University, 1935.

NASH, VERNON. *What is Taught in Schools of Journalism*. Published Master's Thesis, University of Missouri, Journalism Series No. 54, 1928.

"News Notes," *Journalism Quarterly*, VIII (1931), 305.

PULITZER, JOSEPH. "The College of Journalism," *North American Review*, Vol. 178 (1904), 641.

O'DELL, DE FOREST. *The History of Journalism Education in the United States*. Published Doctoral Dissertation, Columbia University, 1935.

OLSON, KENNETH E. "Schools of Journalism and the Press," *Journalism Quarterly*, XVI (1939), 32.

"Problems of Journalism," *Proceedings*, The American Society of Newspaper Editors (1938), 46.

"The Report of the Committee on Schools of Journalism to the A.S.N.E.," *Journalism Quarterly*, VII (1930), 45.

UNPUBLISHED MATERIAL

DAVISON, HERBERT M. "Report of the Schools of Journalism Committee for 1940–41 to the 39th Annual Convention of Southern Newspaper Publishers Association."

POLSON, IZIL I. "Progress in Teaching of Journalism in Colleges and Universities of the United States and an Indication of the Trends Shown." Unpublished Master's thesis, Northwestern University, 1924.

Revised Standards, American Association of Schools and Departments of Journalism, 1941.

"Rules and Precedents of the National Council on Education for Journalism," Mimeographed Bulletin prepared by chairman of The National Council, October, 1938.

APPENDICES

APPENDIX A

COLLEGES AND UNIVERSITIES OFFERING INSTRUCTION IN JOURNALISM IN THE UNITED STATES

GROUP A SCHOOLS

California
University of Southern California, Los Angeles.
Stanford University, Stanford, University.

Colorado
University of Colorado, Boulder.

Georgia
University of Georgia, Athens.

Illinois
Northwestern University, Evanston.
University of Illinois, Urbana.

Indiana
Indiana University, Bloomington.

Iowa
Iowa State College, Ames.
State University of Iowa, Iowa City.

Kansas
Kansas State College, Manhattan.
University of Kansas, Lawrence.

Kentucky
University of Kentucky.

Louisiana
Louisiana State University, Baton Rouge.

Massachusetts
Boston University, Boston.

Michigan
University of Michigan, Ann Arbor.

Minnesota
University of Minnesota, Minneapolis.

Missouri
University of Missouri, Columbia.

Montana
Montana State University, Missoula.

Nebraska
University of Nebraska, Lincoln.

New Jersey
Rutgers University, New Brunswick.

New York
Columbia University, New York City.
New York University, New York City.
Syracuse University, Syracuse.

Ohio
Ohio State University, Columbus.

Oklahoma
University of Oklahoma, Norman.

Oregon
University of Oregon, Eugene.

Pennsylvania
Pennsylvania State College, State College.

Texas
University of Texas, Austin.

Virginia
Washington and Lee University, Lexington.

Washington
University of Washington, Seattle.

Wisconsin
Marquette University, Milwaukee.
University of Wisconsin, Madison.

GROUP B SCHOOLS

Alabama

University of Alabama, Tuscaloosa.

Arkansas

Harding College, Searcy.
University of Arkansas, Fayetteville.

California

College of the Holy Names, Oakland.
Fresno State College, Fresno.
San Francisco State College, San Francisco.
San Jose State College, San Jose.
University of California, Berkeley.
Woodbury College, Los Angeles.

Colorado

Denver University, Denver.
Loretto Heights College, Loretto.
Register College of Journalism, Denver.

Florida

Florida Southern College, Lakeland.
Florida State College for Women, Tallahassee.
University of Florida, Gainesville.
University of Tampa, Tampa.

Georgia.

Emory University, Atlanta.
Mercer University, Macon.

Idaho

University of Idaho, Moscow.

Indiana

Butler University, Indianapolis.
Saint Mary-of-the-Woods College, Saint Mary-of-the-Woods.
University of Notre Dame, Notre Dame.

Iowa

Coe College, Cedar Rapids.
Drake University, Des Moines.
Grinnell College, Grinnell.

Kansas

Baker University, Baldwin City.
University of Wichita, Wichita.

Louisiana

Louisiana Polytechnic Institute, Ruston.
Loyola University of the South, New Orleans.
Tulane University, New Orleans.

Maryland

University of Baltimore, Baltimore.

Massachusetts

Suffolk University, Boston.

Michigan

Marygrove College, Detroit.
Michigan State College, East Lansing.
University of Detroit, Detroit.

Missouri

Washington University, St. Louis.

Nebraska

Creighton University, Omaha.
Hastings College, Hastings.
Midland College, Fremont.

Nevada

University of Nevada, Reno.

New Jersey

Rider College, Trenton.

North Carolina

University of North Carolina, Chapel Hill.

North Dakota

University of North Dakota, Grand Forks.

Ohio

Kent State University, Kent.
Ohio University, Athens.
Western Reserve University, Cleveland College, Cleveland.

Oklahoma

Oklahoma A. & M. College, Stillwater.
Oklahoma Baptist University, Shawnee.
Oklahoma City University, Oklahoma City.

Pennsylvania

College Misericordia, Dallas.
Lehigh University, Bethlehem.
St. Joseph's College, Philadelphia.
Temple University, Philadelphia.
University of Scranton, Scranton.

South Carolina

University of South Carolina, Columbia.

South Dakota

South Dakota State College, Brookings.
University of South Dakota, Vermillion.

Texas
Baylor University, Waco.
Hardin-Simmons University, Abilene.
Mary Hardin-Baylor College, Belton.
Southern Methodist University, Dallas.
Texas Christian University, Ft. Worth.
Texas State College for Women, Denton.
Texas Technological College, Lubbock.
Trinity University, Waxahachie.

Utah
Brigham Young University, Provo.

West Virginia
Bethany College, Bethany.
Marshall College, Huntington.
West Virginia University, Morgantown.

Wisconsin
Mount Mary College, Milwaukee.

Wyoming
University of Wyoming, Laramie.

GROUP C SCHOOLS

Alabama
Alabama Polytechnic Institute, Auburn.

Arizona
University of Arizona, Tucson.

California
San Diego State College, San Diego.
St. Mary's College of California, St. Mary's College.

District of Columbia
The American University, Washington, D. C.
The George Washington University, Washington, D. C.

Florida
University of Miami, Coral Gables.

Georgia
Wesleyan College, Macon.

Illinois
College of St. Francis, Joliet.
Mundelein College for Women, Chicago.

Indiana
Franklin College, Franklin.
Saint Mary's College, Notre Dame, Holy Cross.

Iowa
Cornell College, Mount Vernon.

Kansas
Kansas State Teachers College, Pittsburg.
Washburn College, Topeka.

Kentucky
Murray State Teachers College, Murray.

Maine
University of Maine, Orono.

Massachusetts
Northeastern University, Boston.

Michigan
Albion College, Albion.
Wayne University, Detroit.

Minnesota
College of St. Scholastica, Duluth.

Montana
Billings Polytechnic Institute, Billings.

Nebraska
Union College, Lincoln.

New York
Alfred University, Alfred.
College of New Rochelle, New Rochelle.
Long Island University, Brooklyn.
Saint Bonaventure College, Saint Bonaventure.

North Carolina
Wake Forest College, Wake Forest.

Ohio
Notre Dame College, South Euclid.
Ohio Wesleyan University, Delaware.

Oklahoma
Phillips University, Enid.
Southeastern State College, Durant.
Southwestern State College, Weatherford.

Oregon

Linfield College, McMinnville.
Marylhurst College, Marylhurst.
Oregon State College, Corvallis.

Pennsylvania

Bucknell University, Lewisburg.
Lincoln University, Lincoln University.
Marywood College, Scranton.
University of Pennsylvania, Philadelphia.
University of Pittsburgh, Pittsburgh.
Villa Maria College, Erie.
Westminster College, New Wilmington.

South Carolina

Winthrop College, Rock Hill.

Texas

Howard Payne College, Brownwood.
North Texas State Teachers College, Denton.

Southwest Texas State Teachers College, San Marcos.
Texas Wesleyan College, Fort Worth.
West Texas State Teachers College Canyon.

Utah

Utah State Agricultural College, Logan.

Washington

Eastern Washington College of Education, Cheney.
State College of Washington, Pullman.
Walla Walla College, College Place.

West Virginia

New River State College, Montgomery. (Name changed to West Virginia Institute of Technology in 1941).

Wisconsin

St. Norbert College, West DePere.

GROUP D SCHOOLS

Alabama

Alabama College, Montevallo.
Howard College, Birmingham.
Judson College, Marion.

Arizona

Arizona State Teachers College, Flagstaff.
Arizona State Teachers College, Tempe.

Arkansas

Arkansas A. & M. College, Monticello.
Arkansas College, Batesville.
Arkansas State College, Jonesboro.
Arkansas State Teachers College, Conway.
College of the Ozarks, Clarksville.
Henderson State Teachers College, Arkadelphia.
John Brown University, Siloam Springs.
Ouachita College, Arkadelphia.
Philander Smith College, Little Rock.

California

College of the Pacific, Stockton.
Humboldt State College, Arcata.
Mills College, Oakland.
Mount St. Mary's College, Los Angeles.
Occidental College, Los Angeles.

Pacific Union College, Angwin.
Pasadena College, Pasadena.
Santa Barbara State College, Santa Barbara.
University of Redlands, Redlands.
University of San Francisco, San Francisco.
Whittier College, Whittier.

Colorado

Adams State Teachers College, Alamosa.
Colorado College, Colorado Springs.
Colorado State College, Fort Collins.
State College of Education, Greeley.
Western State College of Colorado, Gunnison.

Connecticut

Albertus Magnus College, New Haven.
University of Connecticut, Storrs.

District of Columbia

Catholic University of America, Washington.
Howard University, Washington.
Miner Teachers College, Washington.
Washington Missionary College, Washington.
Wilson Teachers College, Washington.

Florida

Florida A. & M. College, Tallahassee.
John B. Stetson University, DeLand. (Abolished in June 1940.)
Rollins College, Winter Park.

Georgia

Berry College, Mt. Berry.
Bessie Tift College, Forsyth.
Brenau Colllege, Gainesville.
Georgia State College for Women, Milledgeville.
Oglethorpe University, Atlanta.
Shorter College, Rome.
South Georgia Teachers College, Statesboro.

Idaho

Albion State Normal School, Albion.
College of Idaho, Caldwell.
Lewiston State Normal School, Lewiston.

Illinois

Aurora College, Aurora.
Augustana College and Theological Seminary, Rock Island.
Bradley Polytechnic Institute, Peoria.
DePaul University, Chicago.
Eureka College, Eureka.
Greenville College, Greenville.
Illinois State Normal University, Normal.
Illinois Wesleyan University, Bloomington.
Lake Forest College, Lake Forest.
Loyola University, Chicago.
MacMurray College for Women, Jacksonville.
McKendree College, Lebanon.
Monmouth College, Monmouth.
North Central College, Naperville.
Northern Illinois State Teachers College, DeKalb.
Rockford College, Rockford.
Rosary College, River Forest.
Shurtleff College, Alton.
Southern Illinois Normal University, Carbondale.
The Principia College, Elsah.
Wheaton College, Wheaton.
Western Illinois State Teachers College, Macomb.

Indiana

Ball State Teachers College, Muncie.

Central Normal College, Danville.
DePauw University, Greencastle.
Evansville College, Evansville.
Earlham College, Richmond.
Hanover College, Hanover.
Huntington College, Huntington.
Indiana Central College, Indianapolis.
Indiana State Teachers College, Terre Haute.
Purdue University, Lafayette.
Valparaiso University, Valparaiso.

Iowa

Buena Vista College, Storm Lake.
Clarke College, Dubuque.
Iowa State Teachers College, Cedar Falls.
Iowa Wesleyan College, Mt. Pleasant.
Loras College, Dubuque.
Luther College, Decorah.
Morningside College, Sioux City.
Parsons College, Fairfield.
St. Ambrose College, Davenport.
Simpson College, Indianola.
Upper Iowa University, Fayette.
Wartburg College, Waverly.
Western Union College, Le Mars.
William Penn College, Oskaloosa.

Kansas

College of Emporia, Emporia.
Fort Hays Kansas State College, Fort Hays.
Kansas State Teachers College, Emporia.
Kansas Wesleyan University, Salina.
Marymount College, Salina.
Mount St. Scholastica College, Atchison.
Ottawa University, Ottawa.
Southwestern College, Winfield.
St. Mary College, Leavenworth.

Kentucky

Asbury College, Wilmore.
Bowling Green College of Commerce, Bowling Green.
Eastern Kentucky State Teachers College, Richmond.
Georgetown College, Georgetown.
Kentucky Wesleyan College, Winchester.
Nazareth College, Louisville.
Transylvania College, Lexington.
Union College, Barbourville.
University of Louisville, Louisville.
Western Kentucky State Teachers College, Bowling Green.

Louisiana

Centenary College of Louisiana, Shreveport.
Louisiana College, Pineville.
Louisiana State Normal College, Natchitaches.
Southern University and A. & M. College, Scotlandville.
Southwestern Louisiana Institute, Lafayette.
Ursuline College, New Orleans.

Maryland

Blue Ridge College, New Windsor.
Hood College, Frederick.
Maryland College for Women, Lutherville.
St. Joseph's College, Emmitsburg.
Washington College, Chestertown.
Western Maryland College, Westminster.

Massachusetts

American International College, Springfield.
Atlantic Union College, South Lancaster.
Calvin Coolidge College, Boston.
Eastern Nazarene College, Wollaston.
Emerson College, Boston.
Mount Holyoke College, South Hadley.
Regis College, Weston.
Simmons College, Boston.
Springfield College, Springfield.
State Teachers College, Bridgewater.
Tufts College, Medford.
Wellesley College, Wellesley.
Wheaton College, Norton.

Michigan

Adrian College, Adrian.
Alma College, Alma.
Central State Teachers College, Mt. Pleasant.
Cleary College, Ypsilanti.
Detroit Institute of Technology, Detroit.
Emmanuel Missionary College, Berrien Springs.
Ferris Institute, Big Rapids.
Kalamazoo College, Kalamazoo.
Michigan State Normal College, Ypsilanti.
Northern State Teachers College, Marquette.
Siena Heights College, Adrian.

Minnesota

Augsburg College and Seminary, Minneapolis.
Carleton College, Northfield.
College of St. Catherine, St. Paul.
College of St. Thomas, St. Paul.
Concordia College, Moorhead.
Gustavus Adolphus College, St. Peter.
Hamline University, St. Paul.
Macalester College, St. Paul.
St. John's University, Collegeville.
St. Olaf College, Northfield.
State Teachers College, Bemidji.
State Teachers College, Duluth.
State Teachers College, Moorhead.
State Teachers College, St. Cloud.
State Teachers College, Winona.

Mississippi

Alcorn A. & M. College, Alcorn.
Delta State Teachers College, Cleveland.
Mississippi College, Clinton.
Mississippi Southern College, Hattiesburg.
Mississippi State College, State College.
Mississippi State College for Women, Columbus.
University of Mississippi, Oxford.

Missouri

Central Missouri State Teachers College, Warrensburg.
Culver-Stockton College, Canton.
Lincoln University, Jefferson City.
Lindenwood College, St. Charles.
Missouri Valley College, Marshall.
Southeast Missouri State Teachers College, Cape Girardeau.
St. Louis University, St. Louis.
Teachers College of Kansas City, Kansas City.
William Jewell College, Liberty.

Montana

Carroll College, Helena.

Nebraska

Doane College, Crete.
Duchesne College, Omaha.
Nebraska Central College, Central City.
Nebraska State Teachers College, Chadron.
Nebraska State Teachers College, Kearney.

Nebraska State Teachers College, Wayne.
Nebraska Wesleyan University, Lincoln.
Peru State Teachers College, Peru.
University of Omaha, Omaha.
York College, York.

New Hampshire
Dartmouth College, Hanover.
Keene Teachers College, Keene.
Rivier College, Hudson.

New Jersey
College of Saint Elizabeth, Convent.
Georgian Court College, Lakewood.
New Jersey State Teachers College, Montclair.
New Jersey State Teachers College, Newark.
New Jersey State Teachers College, Jersey City.
Seton Hall College, South Orange.

New Mexico
New Mexico State College, State College.
New Mexico State Teachers College, Silver City.
University of New Mexico, Albuquerque

New York
Brooklyn College, Brooklyn.
Colgate University, Hamilton.
College of Mount St. Vincent, New York City.
City College of New York, New York City.
Good Counsel College, White Plains.
Hartwick College, Oneonta.
Houghton College, Houghton.
Hunter College of the City of New York, New York City.
Nazareth College, Rochester.
Niagara University, Niagara Falls.
Notre Dame College of Staten Island, New York City.
Russell Sage College, Troy.
Sarah Lawrence College, Bronxville.
St. John's College, Brooklyn.
St. Joseph's College for Women, Brooklyn.
St. Lawrence University, Canton.

University of Buffalo (Millard Fillmore College), Buffalo.
University of Rochester, Rochester.
Wagner Memorial Lutheran College, Staten Island.

North Carolina
Elon College, Elon College.
Flora MacDonald College, Red Springs.
Greensboro College, Greensboro.
Lenori Rhyne College, Hickory.
Queens College, Charlotte.
Woman's College of the University of North Carolina, Greensboro.

North Dakota
North Dakota Agricultural College, Fargo.
State Normal and Industrial School, Ellendale.
State Teachers College, Dickinson.
State Teachers College, Fargo.
State Teachers College, Mayville.
State Teachers College, Valley City.

Ohio
Alfred Holbrook College, Manchester.
Antioch College, Yellow Springs.
Ashland College, Ashland.
Baldwin-Wallace College, Berea.
Cedarville College, Cedarville.
College of Mount St. Joseph, Mount St. Joseph.
Denison University, Granville.
De Sales College, Toledo.
Fenn College, Cleveland.
Miami University, Oxford.
Muskingum College, New Concord.
Ohio Northern University, Ada.
Otterbein College, Westerville.
University of Akron, Akron.
University of Cincinnati (Evening), Cincinnati.
University of Dayton, Dayton.
University of Toledo, Toledo.
Ursuline College, Cleveland.
Western College, Oxford.
Western Reserve University, Adelbert College, Cleveland.
Wilberforce University, Wilberforce.
Wittenberg College, Springfield.
Xavier University Downtown College, Cincinnati.
Youngstown College, Youngstown.

Oklahoma

Agricultural and Normal University, Langston.
Catholic College of Oklahoma, Guthrie.
Central State College, Edmond.
East Central State College, Ada.
Northeastern State College, Tahlequah.
Northwestern State College, Alva.
Oklahoma College for Women, Chickasha.
Panhandle Agricultural and Mechanical College, Goodwell.
University of Tulsa, Tulsa.

Oregon

Pacific College, Newberg.
Pacific University, Forest Grove.
Reed College, Portland.
University of Portland, Portland.
Willamette University, Salem.

Pennsylvania

Albright College, Reading.
Allegheny College, Meadville.
Beaver College, Jenkintown.
Cedar Crest College, Allentown.
Chestnut Hill College, Philadelphia.
Dickinson College, Carlisle.
Drexel Institute of Technology, Philadelphia.
Duquesne University, Pittsburgh.
LaSalle College, Philadelphia.
Moravian College, Bethlehem.
Moravian College for Women, Bethlehem.
Muhlenberg College, Allentown.
Pennsylvania College for Women, Pittsburgh.
Rosemont College, Rosemont.
Seton Hill College, Greensburg.
State Teachers College, Bloomsburg.
State Teachers College, California.
State Teachers College, Clarion.
State Teachers College, East Stroudsburg.
State Teachers College, Edinboro.
State Teachers College, Indiana.
State Teachers College, Kutztown.
State Teachers College, Lock Haven.
State Teachers College, Shippensburg.
State Teachers College, Slippery Rock.
State Teachers College, West Chester.
Susquehana University, Sellinsgrove.
Ursinus College, Collegeville.
Washington and Jefferson College, Washington.

Rhode Island

Providence College, Providence.
Rhode Island College of Education, Providence.
Rhode Island State College, Kingston.

South Carolina

Allen University, Columbia.
Claflin University, Orangeburg.
Clemson College, Clemson.
Furman University, Greenville.
Lander College, Greenwood.
Newberry College, Newberry.
State A. & M. College, Orangeburg.

South Dakota

Augustana College, Sioux Falls.
Dakota Wesleyan University, Mitchell.
Northern State Teachers College, Aberdeen.
Sioux Falls College, Sioux Falls.
Yanktown College, Yanktown.

Tennessee

Cumberland University, Lebanon.
King College, Bristol.
Knoxville College, Knoxville.
LeMoyne College, Memphis.
Lincoln Memorial University, Harrogate.
Madison College, Madison College.
Southwestern, Memphis.
State Teachers College, Johnson City.
Tennessee Agricultural and Industrial State College, Nashville.
Tennessee College for Women, Murfreesboro.
Tennessee Polytechnic Institute, Cookeville.
Union University, Jackson.
University of Chattanooga, Chattanooga.
University of Tennessee, Knoxville.

Texas

Abilene Christian College, Abilene.
Agricultural and Mechanical College of Texas, College Station.
East Texas State Teachers College, Commerce.
Houston College for Negroes, Houston.
Incarnate Word College, San Antonio.
McMurray College, Abilene.
Prairie View State College, Prairie View.
Sam Houston State Teachers College, Huntsville.

St. Edward's University, Austin.
St. Mary's University, San Antonio.
Southwestern University, Georgetown.
Sul Ross State Teachers College, Alpine.
Texas College of Arts and Industries, Kingsville.
University of Houston, Houston.
University of San Antonio, San Antonio.
Wiley College, Marshall.

Utah

University of Utah, Salt Lake City.

Vermont

St. Michael's College, Winooski Park.
Trinity College, Burlington.
University of Vermont, Burlington.

Virginia

Lynchburg College, Lynchburg.
Madison College, Harrisonburg.
Mary Baldwin College, Staunton.
Mary Washington College, Fredericksburg.
Roanoke College, Salem.
State Teachers College, East Radford.

Washington

College of Puget Sound, Tacoma.
Gonzaga University, Spokane.
Seattle Pacific College, Seattle.
Western Washington College of Education, Bellingham.

Whitman College, Walla Walla.
Whitworth College, Spokane.

West Virginia

Bluefield State Teachers College, Bluefield.
Concord State Teachers College, Athens.
Davis and Elkins College, Elkins.
Fairmont State Teachers College, Fairmont.
Glenville State Teachers College, Glenville.
Morris Harvey College, Charleston.
Salem College, Salem.
Shepherd State Teachers College, Shepherdstown.
West Liberty State Teachers College, West Liberty.
West Virginia State College, Institute.
West Virginia Wesleyan College, Buckhannon.

Wisconsin

Beloit College, Beloit.
Carroll College, Waukesha.
Milton College, Milton.
State Teachers College, LaCrosse.
State Teachers College, Milwaukee.
State Teachers College, Platteville.
State Teachers College, River Falls.
State Teachers College, Superior.
State Teachers College, Whitewater.

APPENDIX B

GROUP A SCHOOL GRADUATES OVER THREE-YEAR PERIOD

School	1937 Bach.	1937 Mast.	1938 Bach.	1938 Mast.	1939 Bach.	1939 Mast.
Stanford Univ.	30	3	20	1	22	5
Univ. of So. Calif.	19		15		26	
Univ. of Colorado	19		15		14	
Univ. of Georgia	50		45		53	
Northwestern Univ.	58	11	70	8	45	22
Univ. of Illinois	76		102		70	
Univ. of Indiana	19	1	25	1	29	3
Iowa State College	29		29	1	38	1
State Univ. of Iowa	44	6	69	3	37	8
Kansas State College	29		29	1	38	1
Univ. of Kansas	50		59	4	35	
Univ. of Kentucky	28		26		26	
Louisiana State Univ.	22	2	18		22	3
Boston University	21		25		18	
Univ. of Michigan	39	8	29	7	29	7
Univ. of Minnesota	37	2	71	3	58	2
Univ. of Missouri	164	4*	159	10	207	10
Montana State Univ.	15		18		15	
Univ. of Nebraska	18		26		27	
Rutgers University	12		15		21	
Columbia University		60		53		54
New York University	36		29		46	
Syracuse University	12		19		27	1
Ohio State Univ.	28		54		33	
Univ. of Oklahoma	21		28	2	41	1
Univ. of Oregon	36		32		34	
Penn. State College	32		37		35	
Univ. of Texas	28	1	66	2	51	1
Washington & Lee Univ.	6		9		8	
Marquette University	38	1	36	2	42	
Univ. of Wisconsin	56	1	68	5	71	9
Totals............	1,087	102	1,269	103	1,224	128

* Includes one J. D.

138

APPENDIX C

PLACEMENTS FOR 1939 IN GROUP A SCHOOLS

School	Placed on Newspapers	Placed in Allied Flds.	Total Placed	Total Grads.
Stanford University	17	7	24	27
Univ. of So. California	8	8	16	26
Univ. of Colorado	5	2	7	14
Univ. of Georgia	18	30	48	53
Northwestern University	29	18	47	67
Univ. of Illinois		No figures available		70
Univ. of Indiana	11	6	17	32
Iowa State College	4	10	14	18
State Univ. of Iowa	15	14	29	45
Kansas State College	16	11	27	39
Univ. of Kansas	17	6	23	35
Univ. of Kentucky	15	6	21	26
Louisiana State Univ.	12	8	20	25
Boston University	10	1	11	18
Univ. of Michigan	36		36	36
Univ. of Minnesota	15	20	35	60
Univ. of Missouri	133		133	217
Montana State Univ.	8	2	10	15
Univ. of Nebraska	14	2	16	27
Rutgers University	14	14		21
Columbia University	22	32	54	54
New York University		No figures available		46
Syracuse University	7	12	19	28
Ohio State Univ.	9	6	15	33
Univ. of Oklahoma	19	10	29	42
Univ. of Oregon	18	6	24	34
Penn. State College	26	4	30	35
Univ. of Texas	24	8	32	52
Washington & Lee Univ.	6	1	7	8
Univ. of Washington	11	8	19	27
Marquette University	9	16	25	42
Univ. of Wisconsin	20	40	60	80
Totals...............	568	294	862	1,352

APPENDIX D

POPULATION AND TOTAL NUMBER OF NEWSPAPERS, BY STATES

State	Population*	Total Number Newspapers
Alabama	2,809,267	170
Arizona	497,789	52
Arkansas	1,948,268	191
California	6,873,688	757
Colorado	1,118,820	213
Connecticut	1,710,112	91
Delaware	266,505	23
District of Columbia	594,000**	15
Florida	1,877,791	211
Georgia	3,119,953	243
Idaho	523,440	110
Illinois	7,874,155	868
Indiana	3,416,152	413
Iowa	2,535,430	561
Kansas	1,799,137	503
Kentucky	2,839,927	199
Louisiana	2,355,821	134
Maine	845,139	62
Maryland	1,811,546	104
Massachusetts	4,312,332	302
Michigan	5,245,012	449
Minnesota	2,785,896	502
Mississippi	2,181,763	134
Missouri	3,784,664	549
Montana	559,456	136
Nebraska	1,315,834	386
Nevada	110,247	31
New Hampshire	491,524	65
New Jersey	4,160,165	378
New Mexico	531,818	79
New York	13,479,142	808
North Carolina	3,571,623	232
North Dakota	641,935	176
Ohio	6,907,612	530
Oklahoma	2,336,434	374
Oregon	1,089,684	166
Pennsylvania	9,900,180	611
Rhode Island	713,346	24
South Carolina	1,899,804	90
South Dakota	642,961	232
Tennessee	2,915,841	175
Texas	6,414,824	784
Utah	550,310	68
Vermont	359,231	60
Virginia	2,677,773	163
Washington	1,736,191	247
West Virginia	1,901,974	148
Wisconsin	3,137,587	380
Wyoming	250,742	63

* U. S. Census, 1940.
** U. S. Estimate, 1935.

PLACEMENTS FOR 1939 IN GROUP B SCHOOLS

School	Placed on Newspapers	Placed in Allied Flds.	Total Placed	Total Grads.
Univ. of Alabama	16	1	17	19
Univ. of Arkansas	4	1	5	9
Col. of the Holy Names	0	2	2	—
Fresno State College	1	1	2	3
San Jose State Col.	10	0	10	10
Univ. of California	2	2	4	15
Loretto Heights Col.		1	1	1
Florida State Col. for Women	4	3	7	18
Univ. of Florida	8	0	8	11
Emory University	4	7	11	11
Univ. of Idaho	5	2	7	7
Butler University	4	3	7	9
St. Mary-of-the-Woods College	1	0	1	1
Univ. of Notre Dame	12	0	12	24
Coe College	1	0	1	1
Drake University	3	2	5	11
Grinnell College	5	1	6	9
Univ. of Wichita	3	0	3	7
Loyola Univ. of the South	2	2	4	5
Tulane University	3	1	4	13
Marygrove College	5	2	7	9
Michigan State College	18	4	22	22
Washington University	2	1	3	7
Creighton University	3	2	5	5
Midland College	1	0	1	1
University of Nevada	5	0	5	5
Rider College	8	1	9	13
Univ. of North Carolina	12	6	18	34
Univ. of North Dakota	7	2	9	10
Kent State University	5	0	5	5
Ohio University	6	2	8	9
Western Reserve University	2	3	5.	—
Oklahoma A. & M.	3	4	7	10
Lehigh University	2	1	2	5
Temple University	11	4	15	25
Univ. of South Carolina	5	0	5	7
So. Dakota State College	6	0	6	6
University of So. Dakota	1	1	2	3
Baylor University	6	3	9	10
Mary Hardin-Baylor University	0	1	1	2
Southern Methodist University	3	4	7	9
Texas Christian University	3	1	4	6
Texas State College for Women	8	2	10	11
Texas Technological Col.	7	3	10	14
Trinity University	6	3	9	9
Brigham Young University	1	1	2	2
Bethany College	2	0	2	3
Marshall College	2	2	4	4
West Virginia University	7	2	9	16
University of Wyoming	3	0	3	6
Totals...............	238	84	322	475*

* This figure includes two master's degree graduates.

APPENDIX F

DISTRIBUTION OF JOURNALISM PROGRAMS BY STATES

State	Group A Schools	Group B Schools	Group C Schools	Group D Schools	Total
Alabama		1	1	3	5
Arizona			1	2	3
Arkansas		2		9	11
California	2	6	2	11	21
Colorado	1	3		5	9
Connecticut				2	2
District of Columbia			2	5	7
Delaware					
Florida		4	1	2	7
Georgia	1	2	1	7	11
Idaho		1		3	4
Illinois	2		2	22	26
Indiana	1	3	2	11	17
Iowa	2	3	1	14	20
Kansas	2	2	2	9	15
Kentucky	1		1	10	12
Louisiana	1	3		6	10
Maine			1		1
Maryland		1		6	7
Massachusetts	1	1	1	13	16
Michigan	1	3	2	11	17
Minnesota	1		1	15	17
Mississippi		1		7	8
Missouri	1			9	10
Montana	1		1	1	3
Nebraska	1	3	1	10	15
Nevada		1			1
New Hampshire				3	3
New Jersey	1	1		6	8
New Mexico				3	3
New York	3		4	19	26
North Carolina		1	1	6	8
North Dakota		1		6	7
Ohio	1	3	2	24	30
Oklahoma	1	3	3	9	16
Oregon	1		3	5	9
Pennsylvania	1	5	7	29	42
Rhode Island				3	3
South Carolina		1	1	7	9
South Dakota		2		5	7
Tennessee				14	14
Texas	1	8	5	16	30
Utah		1	1	1	3
Vermont				3	3
Virginia	1			6	7
Washington	1		3	6	10
West Virginia		3	1	11	15
Wisconsin	2	1	1	9	13
Wyoming		1			1
Grand Totals	32	71	55	384	542

INDEX

143

INDEX

Group C schools of journalism, defined, 3; course hours offered in, 82; enrollment in, 74; entrance requirements in, 78; graduates of, 82; growth of, 75; list of with dates of origin, 76 ff; number of courses offered by, 80; number of, 74; objectives of, 79; origins and distribution of, 74 ff; program of courses offered by, 77 ff; requirements for graduation in, 79; types of courses offered in, 80 ff; types of organizations in, 78 f; typical program in, 81.

Group D schools of journalism, defined, 3; enrollment in, 88, 102; graduates of, 102; growth of (Graph V), 98; kinds of courses offered in, 101 f; list of, with dates instruction started, 90 ff; logical function of, 99; number of, 88; number of courses offered by, 100; objectives of, 99 ff; origins and distribution of, 88 ff; types of organization in, 99.

Growth of instruction, in journalism in the U.S., 20.

H

Hall, Lemuel E., 31.
Handicaps, of professional schools, 16.
Harper's Weekly, 8.
Harrington, H. F., 23.
Hartford Courier, 30.
Harvard University, 12, 13.
Herbert, H. H., 17.
History, 28.
History and Principles of Journalism, 12.
History of American Journalism, 5.
History of Freedom of the Press, 46.
History of Journalism, 13, 29, 46, 81, 105.
History of Journalism Education in the United States, The, 4.
Household Management, 14.
Hudson, Frederic, 8, 9.
Hyde, Grant M., 23, 26.
Hyde, William, 8.

I

Idaho, University of, 40.
Illinois, 40, 77, 99, 112, 113, 114.
Illinois, University of, 12, 16, 23, 37, 40, 112.
Indiana, 99, 114.
Indiana University, 16, 27, 37.
Influence of the Newspaper, 46, 29.
Inland Daily Press Association, 1, 32.
Institutions, number of, offering journalism in the U.S., 106.

Instruction in journalism, first course of, 7.
Instruction in Journalism in Institutions of Higher Education, 3.
Interpretation, of newspapers and news, 105.
Introduction to Journalism, 81.
Investigation, need for, 121.
Iowa, 40, 61, 77, 99, 112, 113, 114, 115.
Iowa State College, 12, 16, 37.
Iowa, State University of, 44.

J

Jobs, taken by graduates of Group A schools, 50; taken by graduates of Group B schools, 68.
Johnson, H. B., 31.
Johnson, Joseph French, 11.
Joint Committee, organization of, 31; resolution of, 31 f; 107.
Journalism and Society, 46.
Journalism Bulletin, The, 3, 16.
Journalism for Women, 46.
Journalism instruction, dates of origin of (Table 16), 110.
Journalism programs, distribution of during 5-year period, 111.
Journalism Quarterly, 4, 5, 17, 24.
Journalism schools, comparison with other professions, 106.
Journalism Vocations, 46.
Journalistic Writing, 105.

K

Kansas, 40, 114.
Kansas, University of, 11, 16, 27, 37, 40.
Kansas State College, 10, 11, 16, 37.
Kent State University, 66.
Kentucky, 114.
Kentucky, University of, 16.

L

Laboratories, in Group A schools, 54 f; in Group B schools, 71 f; in Group C schools, 86; in Group D schools, 104.
Laboratory facilities, 121.
Latin, 14.
Law, 14, 109; number of accredited schools in, 106.
Law of Journalism, The, 13.
Law of the Press, 29.
Lee, General Robert E., 7, 9, 34.
Lee, James Melvin, 3, 12, 23.
Level of admission, in schools of journalism, 116.
Libraries, in Group A schools, 54.
Library facilities, in Group B schools, 72; in

Group C schools, 86; in Group D schools, 104; in schools of journalism, 121.
Limited programs, 112.
Literature of Journalism, 46.
Literary Aspects of Journalism, 46.
Literary Form of Newspapers, The, 13.
Literature, 28.
Louisiana State University, 16, 37, 40, 114, 115.
Luxon, Norval, Neil, 5; study of 1938, 24.

M

MacNeil, Neil, 5.
McAnally, David Russell, 10.
Magazine and Class Journalism, 12.
Magazines, jobs on by Group A graduates, 50; by Group B graduates, 68.
Magazine Writing and Editing, 27.
Maine, 61, 89, 113, 115.
Maine, University of, 16, 74.
Marquette University, 16.
Mary Washington College, 102.
Massachusetts, 61, 99, 114, 115.
Massachusetts Agricultural College, 16.
Materials of Journalism, 10.
Medicine, 109; number of accredited schools in, 106.
Medill, Joseph, 39.
Medill School of Journalism, 1, 39.
Method, of grouping types of programs, 3.
Michigan, 99, 114.
Michigan, University of, 11, 16, 37, 40.
Minneapolis Tribune, 40.
Minnesota, 99, 114, 115.
Minnesota, University of, 22, 25, 40, 77.
Mississippi, 61, 89, 115.
Missouri Press Association, 12, 38.
Missouri Republican, The, 8.
Missouri, University of, 4, 5, 10, 11, 12, 16, 21, 25, 26, 37, 38, 40, 41, 57, 109, 110, 114; degrees granted by, 49.
Missouri-Yenching Foundation, 40.
Modern Newspaper, 81.
Montana, 98, 114, 115.
Montana State University, 27.
Moon Journal, of Battle Creek, Mich., 31.
Mott, Frank Luther, 5, 109.
Murphy, William J., 40.

N

Nash, Vernon, 4, 21; study of 1928, 24.
National Council on Professional Education for Journalism, 1, 2, 33, 34, 35, 106, 107, 109, 111, 115, 116, 119, 120, 121, 122, 123.

National Editorial Association, 1, 32.
Natural science, 28.
Nebraska, 114, 115.
Nebraska, University of, 11, 16, 37.
Need, most urgent in education for journalism, 115.
Negro college, 74.
Negro schools, 88.
Nevada, 89, 115.
New Hampshire, 61, 89, 115.
New Jersey, 40, 61, 114, 115.
New Jersey Press Association, 39.
New Mexico, 61, 115.
News courses, 47, 64, 80, 81, 118.
News Editing, 29, 81.
News-Gathering, 12.
Newspaper, number of daily and weekly in seven states, 112.
Newspaper Administration, 12, 13.
Newspaper Crusades, 46.
Newspaper Institute, of New Jersey Press Association, 12.
Newspaper Jurisprudence, 12.
Newspaper Making, 12.
Newspaper plants, 54.
Newspaper Problems and Policies, 46.
Newspaper Publishing, 12.
Newspapermen, schools sponsored by, 38 ff.
News Reporting, 81.
News Writing, 101.
New York, 60, 61, 99, 112, 113, 114, 115; meeting of Council in, 34.
New York Evening Post, The, 8.
New York Graphic, 8.
New York Herald, The, 8, 9.
New York Sun, The, 8.
New York Tribune, The, 8.
New York University, 3, 12, 16, 37, 40, 41.
New York World, The, 8, 12.
Nixon, William Penn, 8.
North American Review, 13.
North Carolina, 115.
North Carolina, University of, 16.
North Dakota, 115.
North Dakota, University of, 12, 16.
Northwestern University, 26, 32, 55, 112; five-year plan of, 25 f.
Notre Dame, University of, 16, 57, 74.

O

O'Dell, DeForest, 4.
Office equipment, 12.
Organization, present-types of, in journalism, 115 f.

Ohio, 99, 112, 113, 114.
Ohio State University, 27, 37.
Ohio, University of, 16.
Oklahoma, 114.
Oklahoma, University of, 16, 17, 37, 40.
Olson, Kenneth E., 1, 32, 33, 44, 45.
Oregon, 114, 115.
Oregon State College, 74.
Oregon, University of, 12, 16, 27, 40.
Origin, dates of for instruction in journalism, 19.
Over-supply, of professional schools in journalism, 122.

P

Panhandle, of Oklahoma, 115.
Pattern, of development of curriculum, 11.
Pennsylvania, 60, 61, 77, 89, 99, 112, 113, 114, 115.
Pennsylvania, University of, 8, 16.
Periodical Publishers Association, 34.
Personnel-testing, 29.
Philadelphia Times, The, 8, 11.
Philosophies, of education for journalism, 8.
Philosophy, 28; in education for journalism, 13.
Photography, 54, 71.
Physics, 14.
Pictorial Journalism, 29.
Pittsburgh, University of, 16, 74.
Placement of graduates, by Group A schools, 49; by Group B schools, 67; by Group C schools, 82 f; by Group D schools, 102; total in schools of journalism, 122.
Plain Dealer, 4.
Polson, Izil I., 4, 15.
Population, figures on for seven states, 112.
Pony reports, 71.
Post Standard, 33.
Practical courses, 13.
Practical training, 14, 55.
Pre-journalism training, need for, 107.
Pre-law programs, 106.
Press and Foreign Affairs, 29.
Press and Public Opinion, 29.
Press and World Affairs, 46.
Press, as a social institution, 105.
Press as a Social Instrument, 46.
Press Associations, jobs on by Group A graduates, 50; by Group B graduates, 68.
Press Systems of the World, 46.
Pre-vocational education, 15.

Principles and Standards of Education for Journalism, adoption of, 27.
Printing and Journalism, 14.
Problem of study, 2.
Professional journalism programs, limiting number of, 107.
Professional objectives, 109.
Professions, number of schools serving five, 106.
Professorial rank, 28.
Programs of courses, in schools of journalism, 117.
Program in Teaching of Journalism in Colleges and Universities of the United States and an Indication of the Trend Shown, 4.
Propaganda and Censorship, 46.
Proposed Standards for Journalism Education, 122.
Proposed Standards for Schools of Journalism, 27 ff, 36, 86, 117.
Psychology, 28.
Public Opinion, 25, 46.
Publicity, jobs in by Group A graduates, 50; by Group B graduates, 68.
Publicity office, 71.
Pulitzer, Joseph, 8, 12, 13, 21, 34; endowment of, 38.

R

Radio, 54, 71.
Radio work, jobs in by Group A graduates, 50; by Group B graduates, 68.
Radio Writing and Production, 29.
Rapid expansion, period of, 16.
Recommendations for improvement, 122 ff.
Reid, Whitelaw, 8.
Reinforcement of Existing Departments of Instruction for Benefit of Students in Journalism, 13.
Related studies, 3.
Report on schools of journalism, of 1912, 16; of 1918, 17; of 1928–29, 17.
Reporting, 29, 71.
Requirements for graduation, 117.
Revised Standards, aim of, 35.
Rhode Island, 61, 89, 115.
Roanoke College, 102.
Rutgers University, 12, 39.

S

School of Literature and Journalism, 11.
School newspaper, 54, 71.
School publications, supervision of, 119.
Schools of journalism, concentration of, 114; grouping of, 112.